A NEW KIND

—— OF ——

POWER

USING
**HUMAN-CENTERED
LEADERSHIP** TO DRIVE
**INNOVATION, EQUITY,
AND BELONGING**
IN GOVERNMENT INSTITUTIONS

DARA BARLIN, et al.

A New Kind of Power

Using Human-Centered Leadership to Drive
Innovation, Equity, and Belonging in
Government Institutions

Dedication

To my former bosses from my most formative years, Ellen Moir and Margaret Shelleda, you created the most inspirational environments anyone could have dreamed of being a part of and taught me what true Human-Centered Leadership looks like. To my parents, Mel and Elaine Barlin, for your unyielding support, gentle nudges, and for always creating a psychologically safe environment for me to be who I really am. And finally, to Stacey Halls, our story is the fuel that has been driving my life-long search to make the workplace better.

Acknowledgements & Co-Authors

This book is about the power of the collective over the individual. It seeks to help people learn how to draw on the insights, talents, and ideas of all those in our communities, rather than just focusing in on the one, or the few, who are too often believed to be the sole agents of change. As such, the author seeks to raise up the profile of all of those who have had a meaningful role in shaping this book. These people are more than just contributors. They are co-thinkers, co-cheerleaders, and co-creators. As such, they are being named and recognized as co-authors.

Co-Authors:

My deepest gratitude goes to a special subset of my co-authors, my Awesome Advisory Team. This group of incredible Human-Centered Leaders has offered a never-ending flow of brilliant ideas and moral support while helping me move through the toughest trouble-spots with ease and grace. Thank you for making this process so joyful and meaningful: Ellen Moir, Marla Ucelli, Natalie Brewster Nguyen, Pam Goins, and Shannon Trilli Kempner.

I also want to sincerely thank all the cutting-edge leaders featured in this book for taking a risk to share their stories and strategies with me. The only reason this book exists is because of your pioneering efforts to make government as good as it can be. Thank you for co-authoring the future of Human-Centered Leadership: Alexander Daniels, Ann Maddock, Carmelyn Malalis, Chris Fernandes, Dan Garodnick, Daryl Davis, Dimple Dhabalia, Erica Mohr, Gabriela Hurtado, Gillian Smith, Jen Wick, Keith Richards, Kenyatte Reid, Kip Brooks, Matt Torell, Pam Goins,

Shannon Wheeler Roberts, Vishal 'Victor' Rampaderat, and Yvonne Soto.

I would also like to acknowledge the many fearless government leaders interviewed whose stories did not make it into this book, but who are also doing amazing work and creating wonderful spaces of empowerment in government and beyond.

I am indebted to my community of friends and family who served as readers, feedback givers, focus group members, and cheerleaders pushing my thinking and making invaluable contributions along the journey. It takes a village to write a book, and I am honored to co-author this book with such a wonderful village: Adrienne Cox, Alex Strazzanti, Amy Klassen, Andi Friedman, Dylan Metcalf, Elaine Barlin, Erin-Kate Escobar, Estelle Davis, Bhumika Muchhala, Frances Yasmeen Motiwalla, Guy Powell, Jamie Shay, Jennifer Carman, Joe Aguerrebere, Jon Ramer, Judi Fenton, Julie DeLuca Collins, Kathy Buzad, Kevin O'Gorman, Koren Gains, Matthew Dworkin, Nancy Gannon, Nitzan Pelman, Randall Kempner, Rob Carpenter, Sarah Green, Sharon Braun, ShaRon Rea, Tate Shafer, Wendy Leonard, and Zoe Segal-Reichlin.

Finally, I'd like to thank the Epic Author Publishing team members with whom I worked most closely. Your time, talent, and personalized attention helped ensure all elements of this book came together and allowed us all to provide a meaningful contribution to the field: Trevor Crane (Advisor), Ashley Peterson (Publishing Coach), Alexis Powers (Editor), Daniel Ofem (Formatter), and Fiaz Ahmed (Cover Design).

Contents

Introduction

In 2011, I was sitting in a hotel conference room in San Francisco with several highly regarded policy leaders and philanthropists, otherwise known as mucky mucks. I was trying my best to pay attention to the facilitator who was talking at great length about the latest and greatest federally-mandated education initiative, when I heard him say the five words that would stop my breath and change my life forever.

"Culture eats strategy for breakfast," he said.

This was the first time I heard the quote by management guru Peter Drucker. Apparently, the phrase has been knocked around corporate executive circles for decades. It was a simple concept, but the words shifted my entire perspective on leadership - especially in the government sector.

It finally gave an answer to the questions that had been nagging at me for decades in my work with public institutions. Our government is filled to the brim with brilliant leaders who have giant hearts and incredibly smart ideas for policy to make our communities better. So why weren't we seeing more positive change on the ground? Why weren't we getting more traction in areas like education, housing, transportation, etc.? For the many genius policy initiatives that were being tried out every year in the hopes of making life better for people, why weren't our communities seeing quicker progress?

The answer, it turns out, was staring us right in the face. These five words underscored what most of us have known subconsciously, but maybe not had the proper language to express. When institutions have ineffective culture—meaning when collaboration is difficult, when morale is low, when employee apathy and conflict outstrip passion for the work and derail a unified vision for success—our strategies for positive change suffer enormously.

As soon as I heard the concept explained, I looked around the room and saw many heads nodding. I also heard a few deep sighs. Somebody literally leaned over to me and said, "It's true. But what are you going to do about it?"

My colleague's question was a valid one, but her words got me flustered because she meant it rhetorically. The implication was that nobody in that room believed there was anything to do about it. Instead of engaging in deep conversation, or brainstorming solutions, or sharing best practices on how to create effective culture so that strategies can thrive, the conversation simply moved on to a new topic. It was what it was.

I couldn't let it go, though. I was curious about why this group of powerful change-makers felt helpless against this issue. These particular folks had vast experience moving mountains to get policy passed in all sorts of conditions, persevering in spite of rocks and curve balls being thrown at them on the daily. Yet at the mere mention of the word "culture," everyone threw their hands up in the air and gave up? What was going on?

Was it because culture involves thinking about trust and relationships, and that felt too messy to try to navigate in a workplace context? Was it because the idea of human dynamics lacks a concrete structure that allows leaders to take clear, measurable action to address it? Why did we "yadeyadeyade" over the part about culture if it is so clearly instrumental to our ability to succeed in our mission?

Then it dawned on me. We didn't know how! Although there was a universal agreement among these government leaders that culture is a key driver of organizational success, there was a gap in understanding of how to create that effective culture. Especially with systems steeped in tradition, cherished outcomes like on-time deliverables, and fast-paced metrics of change. Getting powerful leaders to recognize the importance of this issue and take action to address it would not be an easy feat.

I realized that we needed more information. We needed insights on how we could make culture-building easier, more tangible, more actionable, and more metrics-amenable. Perhaps if we could do this, we could help more leaders feel comfortable putting their hands in the dirt and start believing they have the power to build effective culture from the ground up. In doing so, maybe we could collectively lift the quality of our institutions to make our strategies and our policies more powerful and wildly effective. That's when I decided I would spend the next decade of my life seeking to uncover the answer to the question that few had considered asking: How do we make culture-building in government institutions more user-friendly?

My background was well-suited for the task. I had recently gone from a "Type-A" personality to a "Type-Play" personality. Doing so allowed me to keep my love of metrics while granting myself permission to talk about data in ways that were more engaging. So I began digging into the research with great gusto. I started looking for tools to make human dynamics in the workplace feel more concrete and actionable. I sought out ways to measure how nuanced changes in conversation patterns could affect key institutional outcomes. I began working with government agencies by assisting them to strategize and develop programs which supported culture transformation in the workplace. Along the way, I learned two things I didn't expect.

First, some people are extremely reluctant to talk about workplace culture, especially in government institutions. When I first bring up the topic, a swath of people tend to get visibly uncomfortable. Culture means discussing things like relationships, personalities, and emotions. Perhaps there's a fear that if we give permission for folks to discuss feelings at work, someone is liable to take it too far and drive the team off the rails. Many of us have seen it happen. And once emotions come out, they are very difficult to stuff back in. The consensus has been that it is easier to stick with the facts.

But there's also a weird undercurrent of stigma around the topic. Most managers and leaders won't ask for help around creating effective culture because it's assumed that somehow, they are supposed to inherently know how to do it.

This is, of course, a ridiculous concept. It's unreasonable to expect all leaders to automatically know how to create amazing cultures where everyone gets along perfectly and feels valued and supported all the time in the midst of intense time-pressure and change chaos, especially when most of these leaders have never experienced such environments themselves. Yet if a manager or leader admits to not knowing how to build trust on their team, they could be tagged as an incompetent leader—or worse, a bad person. So most managers and leaders simply don't ask for support on these issues. They just keep it to themselves and focus on the deliverables.

The second thing I learned in my quest to make culture transformation feel more concrete is that there are many leaders and managers in government institutions who are already creating powerful thriving cultures. These unsuspecting leaders are designing and implementing strategies that are much more effective than traditional strategies—and they are knocking their outcomes out of the park! But incredibly, these leaders haven't been in the spotlight for the bold initiatives they have been undertaking and the incredible results they've been seeing. Their stories aren't being told.

These powerful leaders tend to have similar traits. Not everyone, of course. But most are personable, with positive dispositions and typically a softer voice. They don't take up a lot of air in meetings and they are always quick to offer support for colleagues whenever a hand is needed. They might not be the most noticeable people in the room when there are many "larger-than-life" personalities nearby, but their game is on point! These masters of human dynamics are creating spaces in government agencies that I didn't believe were possible until I saw them in action with my own eyes.

They are creating super high-performing teams that are producing extraordinarily strong results, seemingly unaffected by the typical problems associated with working in government agencies. They are collaborating with each other and other offices with ease, innovating regularly, addressing equity in meaningful ways, and getting to their goals faster and with more creativity than other teams. Productivity is off the charts, quality of work is outstanding, and they create a spirit of comradery and mutual support that feels infectious. These super-teams are the antithesis of what I had experienced in my time with government agencies, where high-levels of stress, blame-games, and employee apathy ruled the day.

In my quest to answer the driving question that I came up with in that hotel conference room in San Francisco, I made it my business to locate these brave souls who were breaking the norm so I could learn from them. What I gleaned was so powerful, so hopeful, it inspired me to write a book. And here we are! The culmination of this learning, in these pages, for you and all who believe there is potential for our government institutions to be better than they are.

One of the challenges of this process, however, is that I learned a LOT—so much that I couldn't fit it all into one book! So I tackled the issues and strategies that I felt were the most high-leverage, having the potential to create the most positive change while being relatively easy to implement. This would ideally enable those readers who are lit on fire about a topic to move from idea to action in their own environment.

I also created a framework for the chapters so readers could more swiftly move through each one and identify the elements that are of most value to them. Here's a quick overview of the layout.

They each begin with "Let's set the stage." This includes a story of a challenge, usually in a government institution. The story provides the context for the chapter so that readers fully understand the issues that need to be addressed. The stories are all fabricated, but most are based on real-life scenarios to help underscore the seriousness of how these issues affect our government and society at large.

The next section is "Let's unpack the problem." This is where we discuss the WHY? Why is the challenge occurring? What are the root causes? What are the knock-on effects of these issues? This section is where we dive into the background context. We triangulate data from different angles. Sometimes we explore brain science, sometimes we look at organizational development theory, but the primary source of research is based on interviews and focus groups I've done for this book and in my partnership work with government institutions.

In total, over 100 people working in government contexts were interviewed. These primarily include managers and leaders working in city, state, and federal government agencies in the United States. There's also a smattering of front-line workers, elected officials, non-governmental organizations (NGOs) working in partnership with government, international agency staff, and highly-regarded change-makers working? for social good.

In addition, where appropriate, I've added my own personal anecdotes and experiences working in the field of culture transformation within government circles. My own perspective is subjective, and of course does not raise up to the standard of more robust empirical research. But I hope it helps to provide a bit more context and personality to the data presented so it's a more engaging read.

There's one important caveat to keep in mind while you are reading stories from this section. Because of the issue discussed earlier, government agencies are reluctant to talk about culture. To secure permission for agencies to participate, I agreed to the following: to ensure quotes are non-traceable and not recognizable to any reader, quotes about the challenges of culture include pseudonyms and changes to the description details to respect the anonymity of the person and their agency. While quotes are written exactly as they were said, some descriptive details may have been changed to protect the sources. Any resemblance to real people in your office who fit the descriptions is purely coincidental.

The next section is the most hopeful of them all... "Let's solve this together." This portion highlights the promising solutions to the sticky problems discussed in the prior sections. The focus is on concrete strategies that readers can quickly understand and ideally implement to address well-entrenched issues and lift the culture in their own professional environment. Most of the strategies described include examples and compelling stories of managers and leaders in government contexts who are putting these strategies to work. Unlike the previous section, all of the quotes and examples in this section include real names and real details of Human-Centered Leaders who are making the workplace better and seeing great results!

The penultimate section is "Let's wrap it up." The other sections, thus far, are dense with statistics, big ideas, poignant stories, and strategies to support positive change. This short overview helps bring it all together in a quick, pithy summary of the chapter to reinforce the learnings and highlight the key points to remember.

The last and perhaps MOST important element in the whole book is the "Reflective questions for team discussion" at the end of each chapter. This short list of questions is where readers have the opportunity to wrestle with the concepts brought up in the book with their own community. For those who would like a structured approach to facilitating dialogue around the questions, check out the Human-Centered Team-Building Activity we recommend in the Conclusion.

This is the most important part of the book for several reasons. First, it provides an opportunity for people to talk about what they are doing well in this arena already. It's important to honor and celebrate the wonderful leadership strategies that many bring to the table.

It also creates a soft space for hard conversations. By discussing the systemic challenges of culture brought up in various chapters, teams develop a shared language about issues that were once too ambiguous or thorny to discuss. Pathways then open up for people on the team to take action because they have the tools, knowledge, and support of their community behind them. Undercurrents of negativity, resentment, and tension can finally get aired out and often dissolve with the awareness that the team is not alone in facing these hard issues.

These questions are not a cure-all. Be prepared: they can sometimes get difficult because they create a space to finally talk about those intangible challenges and harms that many people in these environments have faced but haven't had a space to talk about previously. The questions have been specifically designed to create a safe and brave space for these discussions to support movement towards trust-building, collective action, and healing. Don't shy away from those hard moments as they are often the most powerful instigators of positive change.

There's no guarantee that everything will tie up in a pretty bow at the end of every discussion. But if the process feels messy and anyone on the team takes action, you are probably doing it right. If people feel safe enough to be authentic and finally speak their truth in ways people can hear and understand, you will be creating the conditions for progress.

And if the strategies you consider provide a sense of hope that everyone can work together to lift the culture, then you are well on your way to being Human-Centered Leaders laying the foundation for innovation, equity, and belonging.

Chapter One

Designing Systems to Support More Choice and Voice

Let's set the stage...

Do you remember that classic "I Love Lucy" episode where Lucy and Ethel are working at the chocolate factory? The manager comes in and bellows that if even one chocolate slips by without being wrapped, they will be fired on the spot. As the conveyor belt starts picking up speed, they can't keep up and in an act of desperation start stuffing their hats and mouths so they won't get in trouble. When they see their manager coming back, they swallow what they can and hide the rest of the missed chocolates down their shirts. The ruse works. Clearly pleased with Lucy and Ethel's "success," the manager believes they can take on a bigger load and directs the conveyor belt controller to "speed it up!"

First aired on TV in 1952, this iconic skit has stood the test of time. It STILL makes people laugh. Comedy is supremely well-suited at revealing our shortcomings. In this case, it's great at showing us why so many of our government institutions are, sadly, set up to fail. And not the "good" kind of fail, where something valuable is learned and the institution grows from the experience. It's the "bad" kind of fail, where taxpayer dollars get wasted, drama ensues, and smart policy initiatives fly off the rails like unwrapped chocolates.

This happens because some government institutions are set up like traditional factories. People at the top, with elected or appointed positional power, come up with the ideas to support the institutional goals. They task those underneath them—middle managers—with creating an implementation plan to roll out the ideas. Those middle managers tell those underneath them—the front-line workers—what to do and how to do it. Voila! The end product or service is ready for distribution.

This system only works, however, if there is strict compliance with all the orders and directions given by those from the top. If any employees in the factory line don't get the deliverable out of the gate in the timeline dictated, it messes up the whole assembly line. To keep the line moving forward, some leaders have used a "Command and Control" style of leadership to ensure strict adherence to top-down orders.

In this model of leadership, fear is used as one of the primary methods of motivation to keep the assembly line intact. If an employee misses a deadline, questions a policy, makes a mistake, or tries out a different idea for how to roll out a strategy, they may face harsh consequences. These penalties could include threats to their job security, including: having a damaging letter added to their file, having work taken away, or getting fired. Or they could include more shame-based threats that damage their confidence and sense of self, such as getting called out harshly in public, or being talked down to in front of peers.

All of these consequences create a sense of dread among employees in these environments. Most will go to great lengths to avoid doing anything that could disrupt the assembly line and risk getting them in trouble. As a result, front-line workers and even some middle managers will typically not speak up when they believe they can't get something done or when they see a plan going off the tracks. Instead, they ignore the glitches in the system, pretend they know more than they do, and do whatever they can to hide their mistakes. They are metaphorically (and in the case of Lucy and Ethel, literally) swallowing the information that is keeping the organization from being successful.

Funny on TV. Not funny in our government institutions.

There are a number of people who have sought to change this dynamic and inspire a healthier and more effective leadership structure. The challenge is, most leaders in our government systems are so accustomed to the old way of behaving, they see no problem with it!

To be fair, that perspective is understandable. At first, the old way of doing things was very helpful. When it was originally set up, "Command and Control" provided a quick and efficient way of constructing systems of organization that ensured citizens received critical services.

Employees appeared motivated because they continued to show up to work for the paycheck. And government programs moved forward, assuming that what lower-level employees felt was irrelevant.

In addition, there are specific times when a "Command and Control" style of leadership is still helpful. For example, in true emergency situations where group panic is setting in, like a bomb scare, having one strong voice to dictate steps to safety can feel comforting.

Yet current research suggests that using this method of leadership as the de facto management style on a daily basis is both counterproductive and dangerous. If left unchecked, it will stifle innovation, kill culture, scare talent away, reinforce inequity, and woefully reduce outcomes over the long term for both staff and the communities being served.

Let's unpack the problem...

Not every government institution uses a "Command and Control" leadership style. However, the ones that do often suffer from a slew of headaches that take humans and policies off-track. Some of the most typical symptoms of a "Command and Control" culture include: employee disengagement, high absenteeism, conflict, gossip, fractioning of employees into "sides," and poor implementation of policy. This section explores some of the biggest root causes for these issues so that we can offer more effective solutions to resolve them in the next section.

Red Shiny Button

My niece and I went to the Children's Museum in Chicago a few years ago. As we were walking in, there was this giant red button with a sign that said, "DO NOT PRESS THIS RED SHINY BUTTON." Want to guess how many people pressed the button? You got it! The vast majority. It was estimated that upwards of 80% of people who read the sign pushed the button. The museum was obviously playing with us. By telling us we can't press the button, we want to press it. This tricky brain phenomenon is later described as *Reactance Theory.*

Reactance is the negative knee-jerk reaction our brains feel when we perceive someone is giving us instructions to do something that we have not yet bought into. Our brain perceives that someone is trying to take away our sense of agency or freedom. This feels like an attack on our personhood which activates the amygdala part of our brain and puts us in fight or flight[1] (survival) mode. Simply put, reactance is the idea that nobody likes being told what to do—and when we are told what to do without our consent, we want to do the opposite.

In traditional "Command and Control" environments, many middle managers and most front-line employees are being told what to do and have learned they don't have much choice or voice in the matter. If they are tasked with something they don't believe will be useful or didn't have any say in helping to design, they will probably not want to do it and be frustrated that they have to do it. But inevitably they will do it, because they need the job and don't want to face harsh consequences.

Instead of pushing back or speaking their truth, most simply bite their tongue. This causes many to silently stew on the inside. As a result, most employees feel unheard at best, and unappreciated or disrespected at worst.

According to a recent Gallup poll, 85% of employees around the world hate their job (70% in the U.S.).[2] Another study showed that most people trust strangers more than they trust their boss.[3] The current state of the workplace is broken, and yet very few leaders at the top levels of agencies are talking about it. There are a few reasons for this.

One reason is that when leaders get promoted into higher-level positions, without realizing it, their capacity for empathy is reduced. That's not a dig against their character—it's brain science. Power literally creates brain damage that makes those in senior positions less interested in listening to those with lower-level status.[4] It has nothing to do with whether someone is a good person or not. It is merely a function of being human. Unless there is a concerted effort and/or an explicit system in place to maintain it, our physiology determines that most of us will lose empathy for those below us as we gain influence in our organizations. At an institutional level, that means there is inherently less value placed on listening to employee ideas and suggestions at lower levels of the organization.

Another big reason is that managers often don't even know when there is a problem. That's because employees generally don't feel free to speak up when they are feeling frustrated. We are trained from when we are young to keep our mouths shut so we stay in good favor with our superiors. So instead of telling management when there's an issue, employees tend to avoid the boss altogether and just gossip to each other. It's a no-win situation for managers. If they don't know where there are issues because no one is willing to speak up, there is no way to resolve those issues.

The interesting thing is that on an aggregate level, employee gripes and frustrations tend to be similar across the board, regardless of the institution. Here are a few stories that highlight some of the most common refrains from employees describing their experience about choice and voice.

This is Mary, a front-line worker from a government agency in a small midwestern town, talking about her experience feeling undervalued. She suggests:

> "A lot of the work comes from the top down. People on the ground have great ideas... but you don't feel like your ideas are valued. You are not being heard. It makes you feel like you're just a cog in the wheel—like your opinions and who you are doesn't matter."

Mary goes on to describe her frustration that the people closest to the communities who are being served often have powerful insights about how to improve services in ways that lead to better distribution of services, "but those insights usually fall on deaf ears." As a result, employee engagement goes down and the number of missed opportunities for positive change goes up.

Designing Systems to Support
more Choice and Voice

Some employees try to offer their suggestions, but in politically charged environments, trying can be painful. Michael, a middle manager in a medium-sized city on the East Coast, puts it this way:

> *"People try to take initiative, but sometimes get their hand slapped. That discourages them from trying anything in the future."*

Michael explains that in his office a hand slap means getting blasted on a full-team email with many peers, or being scolded in ways that feel like you're 7 years old and your dad is yelling at you. While none of these slaps are necessarily job-threatening, he suggests that the fear of being talked down to or humiliated in a professional context is strong enough to kill the spirit of innovation in many employees. Why would they try to improve anything if they are likely to get shamed for the effort?

Even though most managers are seeking to empower their staff, there is sometimes a lack of knowledge about how to give feedback in ways that feel supportive, rather than demeaning. When employees are told that their ideas are off-base without any exploration of the idea, and especially when that message comes across in a way that feels shameful, it will often put the kybosh on employee trust, desire to take initiative, and ability think outside the box in the future. Because some managers aren't aware of these human dynamics and few are taught this nuanced detail during their training, the practice of sidelining employee ideas continues in some spaces.

There is also an element of hierarchy in government institutions that demands only people "at the right level" should be present for certain meetings. Leaders meet with leaders, middle managers with middle managers, etc. Overstepping this hierarchy can be felt as a slap in the face to people in more powerful positions and cause problems. But reinforcing this dynamic means that institutions are losing opportunities to engage employees and see the holes in their plans.

Ben, a highly skilled middle manager in an IT division of a government agency in the Southwest, wreaked havoc in his department when he asked some of his direct reports working on the front-line to attend important meetings with him. His superiors told him it was not appropriate to bring in junior staff, and he would get written up if he kept doing it. He asked them:

"How is it not appropriate to bring in the people who will be most affected by the policy? Don't you think they might have some good ideas since they have the most interaction with the people actually using our services?"

Ben says his supervisors didn't take well to his questions. He decided to go to the mat on this issue and ended up getting a letter in his file, rather than adhering to the top-down tradition of "Command and Control." Less than a year later, Ben left the organization.

The Macro Effects of Micro-Sabotage

When employees are feeling frustrated that they are being told what to do without honoring their voice, and don't feel safe sharing those frustrations, their anger will often come out in other ways. These manifest through small actions called "micro-sabotage." Usually, no one is intentionally trying to ruin the institution or engage in full-on mutiny. Rather, it's how each person deals with the reactance and cognitive dissonance stemming from not feeling heard. At the individual level, these actions don't manifest themselves in much damage. But when done in the aggregate, with lots of people performing small acts of micro-sabotage all of the time, it can have a devastating impact on the overall effectiveness and mission of the agency.

Micro-sabotage can range in how it appears. Some employees will do the work they are told to do but perform it reluctantly. Either they drag their feet and/or don't put a lot of care into their work. That means the quality of their work is much lower than what it could be. As a result, the end product is less timely and less effective.

Others will just do the bare minimum and avoid change at all costs, holding on to old practices and refusing to try anything new. Still others will find excuses to not come into work, which makes it hard on the team and reduces overall productivity.

The irony is that most government institutions tend to be filled with smart, passionate people who go into the field because they want to do good in their community. But over time in challenging cultures, that passion wanes, apathy sets in, and government then gets the unenviable reputation for housing "lazy bureaucrats" that reduces effectiveness and does damage to public trust.

Turf Wars, Favoritism, and Backstabbing

Another problem with the old traditional "Command and Control" style of leadership is that it creates a scarcity mindset among staff. Nobody likes being told what to do, but if you grin and bear it and have the fierce determination to claw your way high enough to the top of the organization, you can attain one of the very few positions at the very top of that ladder and get a hold of the "brass ring"—being able to tell *other* people what to do! It is the ultimate power exchange.

The unintentional consequences of this sad, but very human, scarcity mindset are disastrous. A number of problematic behaviors begin to emerge that reduce quality, reinforce inequity, and make human emotions explode in dramatic fashion all over the organization. This drama has the power to thwart or kill any policy initiatives underway.

In "Command and Control" environments, this type of behavior is hard to get around for a few reasons. First, it leads to what many of us call "yes-circles"—where people say yes to those in power all of the time instead of pushing back or speaking their truth. Yes-circles occur because the stronger relationships you have with people in power, the more likely you are to secure a leadership position. You are more likely to maintain those beneficial relationships if you are willing to support—and not challenge—their ideas.

This creates a phenomenon where leaders (usually unintentionally) surround themselves with people who say "yes, great idea" a lot of the time. The problem this creates is that short-sighted ideas sometimes get moved through the pipeline. It also means that people at the middle-top don't feel empowered to push back when faced with unrealistic timelines and insufficient infrastructure for rollout of initiatives. This of course makes it less likely that initiatives will be successful, reduces trust with those expected to implement policies, and costs the institution millions of taxpayer dollars in inefficiency and waste. But leaders often don't know it because those under them have a scarcity mindset—they are too scared of losing their positional power to speak their truth.

Scarcity mindset also leads to an almost impenetrable tendency towards "turf wars." James, a leader in a large urban government agency, suggests that:

> *"We really have to figure out how to get rid of the 'stay in your lane' mentality... figuring out how to work with other divisions who have other priorities."*

Addressing James's concern is hard, though. The act of collaborating with other departments or government agencies is complex and slow, and makes it harder to achieve the expectation of rapid-paced metrics of success. The fear of being seen as a less effective leader in the short-term is strong enough to overpower the benefits of working together over the long-term. Instead, a spirit of cutthroat competition arises, and a spirit of collaboration and systems efficiency become the big losers.

This drought mentality also creates the perfect conditions for internal conflict and unnecessary drama. If you can get ahead and win favor with the more senior level officials by badmouthing those from other divisions who aren't in the inner-circle, or who are temporarily not in good standing with those in the inner-circle, some people seeking influence will take that opportunity—even though it means throwing colleagues under the bus. This fosters a fair amount of blame-gaming, where people point fingers at others in the institution rather than taking responsibility and learning from the mishaps. This sets the stage for a number of behaviors associated with a *Real Housewives-* and *House of Cards*-level of drama, including: infighting, gossip, revenge mindset, credit-stealing, rumor mills, and backstabbing.

This behavior usually does not start out as mean-spirited or intentional. In cutthroat government environments, backstabbing is merely an act of survival. As Miguel, a leader in a government agency on the Southeastern seaboard, put it:

> *"People who are cut down but manage to get promoted, then turn around and cut down others because, you know, if they went through it... others should have to too. It's really just trauma repeating itself."*

The drama continues into the world of hiring and promotions. In hierarchical organizations, there are only a few positions at the top. That's the nature of hierarchy! Especially in politically-charged organizations, the most leaders want the people around them to be people they can trust. This means they tend to choose their team based on who they like and who they know can do the work. This makes sense, right? Better to go with people you know than people who are wild cards and could bring down everything you've worked to create. This is why 80% of jobs are based on personal and professional connections.[5] You want to be able to trust the people BEFORE you hire them, to hedge your bets.

This tendency, unfortunately, quickly leads to favoritism because leaders naturally pick candidates they are familiar with to surround them at the upper echelons of management. This is great for building a team you can count on but abysmal for creating a fair process where all people have access to power. Instead, it reinforces what LinkedIn CEO Jeff Weiner calls the "Network Gap." The fewer social networks or connections you have to those in power, the less likely you'll ever be able to access that power—no matter how superb your skills or work ethic.

If you've read this far, you may be feeling discouraged. The problem of "Command and Control" culture in government might be so deep and entrenched that it feels overwhelming and deflating. Fear not! Luckily, this is a solvable problem! And it's not that hard or expensive to fix. In fact, a LOT of government leaders have figured out the formula for change—and are seeing some fabulous results.

Let's solve this together...

Instead of relying on the old traditional "Command and Control" method of management, a new brand of leaders are using the "Engage and Inspire" method, sometimes referred to as the Human-Centered approach. This approach doesn't eliminate hierarchy, nor does it demand a huge turnover in leadership. The method just creates better structures for empowering all voices within the institution. It's better at listening to the least-heard voices, giving employees more choices in their workflow, and being nimble enough to change based on what is being learned from their staff.

The shift is not expensive or hard to create, but it does require a change in mindset. Rather than seeing employees simply as vehicles for moving forward ideas that come from the top, the new mindset invites leaders to see them as valuable partners in the work of creating change. Instead of focusing on compliance-like protocols that tell employees what to do and how to do it, it focuses on asking employees their opinions and learning from their responses.

This change in approach might sound minor to some, but make no mistake—it is transformative for any organization. It will swiftly shift the concentration of power from one direction (top-down only), to a multi-directional (top-down, bottom-up, and across) flow of leadership potential. Once that shift occurs, trust starts to be built at every level of the organization and a sense of excitement and belonging takes hold.

That strong sense of belonging isn't just a feel-good mushy-gushy outcome. It leads to tangible results that have powerful implications for government institutions. According to *Harvard Business Review*, a strong sense of employee belonging leads to a 56% increase in job performance, a 50% drop in turnover risk, and a 75% reduction in sick days. For an organization with 10,000 people this results in annual savings of more than $52 million.[6]

There are additional benefits. Because the "Engage and Inspire" process encourages more bottom-up and across flows of information, leaders receive more regular information about the people doing impressive work on the ground instead of just those who are savvy at navigating into the inner circle. That acknowledgement of who is doing notable work often changes the composition of those who have access to senior-level positions. This significantly reduces favoritism in the hiring process and creates leadership pathways for those who have not historically had a voice in decision-making. That means government institutions naturally become more equitable and inclusive, while also finding and promoting more effective leaders. We'll talk more about this in Chapter 5.

Finally, because employees are feeling heard and valued, many begin to branch out and offer suggestions that support small and large innovations. This enables government agencies to engage in regular improvement efforts that support more effective and efficient systems, with bigger positive results for policy efforts and the communities being served. This comes up a lot in Chapter 2.

All in all, by focusing on lifting employee voices, government organizations can wildly increase innovation, equity, and belonging. We'll explain exactly how to do this. But first, a caveat.

CAVEAT: The Solution is Not a "Suggestion Box" or an "Open-Door Policy"

True "Engage and Inspire" workplace environments require genuine structures for deep listening. Superficial "listening" mechanisms like suggestion boxes or open-door policies are often woefully inadequate for stimulating the change needed to make initiatives better.

For example, let's say Kiara is a middle manager responsible for reading employee suggestions in her agency's suggestion box. She likes reading them and even believes some are good ideas. Unfortunately, Kiara has a lot on her plate already and doesn't have the capacity, political will, or skills to be able to champion these suggestions from idea into reality.

The laws of motivation say unless the idea is her own, Kiara is unlikely to do all the heavy-lifting required to get someone else's idea off the ground. So the insights in the suggestion box remain nice ideas on the periphery of the organization, but they usually never see the light of day (unless someone more senior takes notice and chooses to put their weight behind it).

Similarly, open-door policies sound great and can be wonderful for addressing small-scale, quick-fix problems. But unless there is an explicit and intensive effort to create psychological safety in the organization (see Chapter 3), most employees will be too afraid to go into a leader's office and tell them the honest truth about a policy they think is misguided.

Even if an employee was bold enough to push back on an idea, the leader is unlikely to make major modifications to an important policy because of the complaint of one disgruntled employee. Nor should they! One person is one data point, not a pattern. If that's the only data point available, it's not reliable enough to warrant a big change in the structure of the organization. Open-door policies are therefore insufficient for putting a finger on the pulse of the systemic factors getting in the way of policy implementation, and inadequate for supporting large-scale improvement.

By contrast, if a leadership team is committed to creating a truly Human-Centered approach, where there is deep listening of all employees across the board—and a willingness to not just listen, but to change the way things are done—THEN all the benefits of trust, innovation, and an inspired workforce will quickly begin to accrue. To get there, government institutions need _to choose to become_ a learning culture by engaging and inspiring all of their employees to speak up.

If you aren't sure how to do that, have no fear. Lots of leaders have begun moving in this direction. Here are some leadership strategies they've been using to foster an "Engage and Inspire" culture in government agencies across the country.

1. Co-Crafting Policy Solutions

Perhaps the most high-leverage strategy for creating a fully engaged and inspired workforce is collective goal-setting and strategic planning. This means not waiting 'til the higher-ups figure out all the details and are asking for feedback later, but instead including everyone who is affected by a policy or practice within an organization to take part in the design of the policy or decision-making from the beginning.

In addition to making employees feel heard and valued, this strategy ignites employee passion for whatever changes are coming because they feel they had a hand in creating it. It gives them a sense of ownership and pride in the work. It also has the added benefit of identifying and addressing potential implementation pitfalls that might otherwise be blind spots for decision-makers in more traditional senior offices.

At first, this new type of approach may feel daunting, considering the wacky notion of including all employee voices, with all of the varying ideologies, personalities, and ideas in one decision-making process. It feels like such a method could create chaos and conflict rather than a unified vision of success. Yet there are a number of models that are gaining traction in government circles. These models are making the process work smoother and more efficiently than newbies to the process would anticipate. Here are just a few of the collective policy development strategies that are currently being used to support this work.

Dotmocracy[7] Method

At its core, Dotmocracy is a simple method of voting with stickers (usually with "sticky dots") that allows people in groups to engage in rapid decision-making to help prioritize big ideas. In this context, the strategy is used to bring a group of people together, representing a subset of all the employees and stakeholders who would be affected by a potential policy shift. This includes front-line workers, middle managers, leaders and, if possible, even community members and prospective policy funders. We recommend no more than 30 people in the group (though you can always repeat this process as many times as you like to get more people involved.[8])

A leader or an experienced facilitator presents the group with a single problem that is thwarting institutional outcomes. Ideally, research is provided first to help better understand the extent and root causes of the problem. Then the group brainstorms (or is presented with a predetermined list of potential solutions) to address the problem.

Some groups allow participants to do a quick advocacy round to articulate why one particular solution is important to them. Each participant is given a set of sticky dots (usually between 3-5) and uses weighted polling[9] to vote on which solutions they feel are strongest based on criteria set by the group. Afterward, the group tallies the results to identify the winning solution(s). Leaders then commit to rolling out the winning solution(s) (either via pilot or at scale). If time permits, the group can even offer insights to leaders about how to roll out the winning solution(s) in ways that are likely to foster the highest levels of success.

The process usually takes between one and three hours and is very simple to apply. But don't let the simplicity of the process fool you. It has the power to engage and unite people from all parts of the institution in ways that inspire a common vision for success and a passion for collective action to achieve that vision.

Case in point, Pam Goins, the former Executive Director for Women in Government, hosted a roundtable discussion with Republican, Democratic, and Independent state legislators from across the nation. During one roundtable that I was privy to, the group focused on addressing the mental health and opioid addiction issues that were escalating in many of the states represented by the participants. This was a tough issue, so Pam brought in a wealth of resources including NGO leaders, community members affected by the issue, expert facilitators, and potential funders of future initiatives.

Rather than getting bogged down in ideological clashes that might inhibit policy movement on the topic, she and her facilitators used Dotmocracy to build trust across party lines and come to solutions based on consensus. Pam set the stage by articulating the severity of the problem nationally and gave the NGOs and community members a platform to share their research and perspectives. The facilitator then gave everyone five sticky dots and broke the participants into small ideologically-mixed groups with 10 minutes to come up with potential solutions. Each group wrote their solutions on chart paper on the surrounding walls and shared why they thought their particular solution would be successful.

Designing Systems to Support more Choice and Voice

The larger group came up with criteria for how to guide their thinking in the weighted voting process. Their criteria included the following:

(1) What solution would make the biggest positive impact?
(2) What would be most policy-amenable, meaning easiest to get passed in their state?
(3) Which were they most passionate about and willing to go to the mat for?

Note that likely no single solution would meet all three criteria. The criteria are meant to serve as a mental guide to support decision-making and remind us that there are always tradeoffs when crafting policy. It's not a checklist to find the one perfect solution. It's up to each participant to choose the tradeoffs that are most meaningful to them.

Each participant had time to walk around, review all of the potential solutions on the walls, and put their five sticky dots on the solutions that they felt best met the criteria from their perspective. Then they took a step back to view the visual representation of the dots and tallied the results.

The visualization and tangible elements of the activity was key because it helped everyone physically see and feel the collaborative process. It wasn't happening in an office somewhere else or on a piece of technology that was one-step removed. They were finding a solution together, right then, right there. In effect, they had turned a regular humdrum conference room into what Lin-Manuel Miranda described as "the room where it happens." That powerful energy inspired a sense of individual ownership and collective pride when the results came in.

In the end, the group achieved consensus on a solution to support success, which Pam subsequently documented and created an initiative around. The participants left feeling energized and empowered that they had engaged in bi-partisan efforts in a way they hadn't felt prior to the event. Even those participants whose vote didn't make it to the winning solution said they walked away feeling valued, heard, and excited that a group of people from such different perspectives were able to reach consensus so quickly. One legislator remarked, "it was the best facilitation [she]'d ever seen."

In the current state of polarization in U.S. politics, this quick and easy system of bringing people together to create meaningful change felt transformative and hopeful. All it took was a leader who understood the power of structured conversations and some sticky dots.

Participatory Budgeting

Participatory budgeting is an emerging process now used by government agencies in the United States, France, Germany, Bolivia, Canada, Kenya, and scores of government agencies around the globe. The method sets aside a specific amount of money and then enables employees and/or community citizens to develop proposals for how to use the money to improve the community. Individuals and small groups come up with projects for how to spend the money and advocate for their projects within the larger group. The larger group then votes for their project of choice and the winning ideas get funded and implemented by the government organization.

One of the best elements of this approach is that the communities themselves discuss and identify priorities based on need. This tends to help community members better articulate and get their needs met while drawing out empathy and connection across groups in some spaces. New York City (NYC) Councilman, Brad Lander, talks about his experience using the strategy:

> *"One thing we saw was a real balance between self-interest and people's community spirit. That's a great part of democracy, you need both to have it work."*

The councilman's project included community members of a school district in Brooklyn, NY engaging in a participatory budgeting process for a new project to support school improvement. Some of the more affluent parents proposed things like new computers and outdoor learning labs. Another group of parents proposed a project to put doors on student bathroom stalls where there had been none previously.

The doors project won the funds with an overwhelming majority. That's because it shed a light on the basic needs of some in the community that weren't on other people's radar screen. Some of the parents whose project ideas didn't get funded were fully on board. It just didn't seem right funding fancy technology when there were students who were being robbed of their dignity daily.

The project works because when people have the opportunity to see the reality of inequitable distribution of resources with their own eyes, many times, empathy will shine through.

2. Modify the Composition of the Leadership Team

Most government cabinets or leadership teams comprise seasoned veterans who have a track record of doing excellent work and are in close proximity to the "inner circle." To make the process of decision-making fair and inclusive, it's essential to include the voices of those who are doing good work but aren't yet on the radar of those in the "inner circle." Here's a few ways to accomplish this:

Ad Hoc Cabinet Members

Some government institutions are transforming the composition of their cabinets. Just like some school boards have a member of the student body on their board, cabinet members can bring in new, fresh voices of front-line workers onto their cabinet every time there is a new initiative. Doing this ensures senior-level policymakers are keeping their finger on the pulse of what is reasonable and realistic to expect. Rather than rolling out initiatives with overly ambitious timelines that lead to ineffective implementation, poor outcomes, and undesirable culture, these ad hoc cabinet members can advise on creating schedules that are manageable and help create the infrastructure for initiative success that exceeds expectations. At the same time, these cabinet members can suggest new ideas that create "out-of-the-box thinking" and help spark innovations with powerful outcomes.

For example, Governor Easley of North Carolina brought in Ann Maddock, a middle school teacher, to serve alongside him on his cabinet on all issues related to education. When Ann told him about the conditions in schools that educators face, he empowered her to find a solution. She proposed doing a state-wide school working conditions survey. Many education leaders in the state balked at the idea because it seemed like a political hot potato and a logistical nightmare filled with headaches. But because of the governor's commitment and belief in the voices of teachers, the first statewide survey in the country about teaching conditions was soon underway in 2002.

Using a method similar to a Dotmocracy, Ann and her team brought all the stakeholders together, from principals to district leaders, teachers, and parents. Together they co-created a plan and did the work to build trust across the community and make it happen. Then the governor made real changes to policy based on the results of the survey. Two decades later, it is considered one of the most valuable contributions to the rise in the quality of schools in North Carolina. As many as 19 states followed North Carolina's lead and instituted their own statewide survey of teachers to gather input on ways to improve teaching conditions. Today, the survey boasts a teacher response rate of a whopping 91% across the state, and that means teachers feel like they have a voice in decisions that affect them.

Initiative Think Tanks

Prior to rolling out initiatives, invite those responsible for pushing the implementation through from the middle to the front-lines to "pressure test" it. Engage them in meetings to identify potential obstacles, design implementation plans, consider unintended consequences, and explore creative alternatives that help to make the initiative better. Then follow through by communicating how they improved the initiative across the organization so they get credit for their participation.

27

Designing Systems to Support
more Choice and Voice

The processes described above are not hard to invoke, but they can sometimes get messy. And that's a good thing! For example, Senior Design Manager at the Port of Portland, Jen Wick, was tasked with creating visuals for the institution's Shared Prosperity Through Social Equity Initiative. This was a slight deviation from the expected template, and—given the sensitive topic—she wanted to get it right. Rather than assuming she and her team had all the answers, her team created a think tank process to invite consensus and feedback from their most diverse employee groups. She and her team did presentation and feedback sessions with Employee Resource Groups representing different voices at the Port, including BIPOC and LGBTQIA groups, as well as all the staff working within the Diversity Program. They received lots of meaningful feedback that helped inform and support powerful visuals for the initiative.

However, engaging in the process didn't provide clear-cut answers. In fact, the process reinforced for her that even within these groups, there are many voices and perspectives. The feedback allowed her and her team to weigh the tradeoffs in more nuanced and helpful ways. Perhaps even more importantly, Jen suggests it provided the employees in the organization with a stake in the initiative. She says, "it enabled them to feel agency and access to the work that my team was doing. That builds trust and partnership that will pay dividends for years to come." Jen offers that the way things are done are just as important as what gets done. She continues:

> "It was a strong reminder that when we invite different voices to view and comment on our process, we grow our skills as collaborators while building relationships. That's always a part of our goals. The results are at times surprising. And the process consistently pushes us to do the work we are here to do—communications that speak effectively to the public with inclusion at the center."

3. Transform Current Practices

There are a number of strategies organizations currently use to support employee voice. Unfortunately, because of lack of time and capacity to implement changes, these methods often lead to interesting "aha!" moments, or good conversation after reading a bullet point in a report, but rarely result in deep, lasting change. Part of the issue is that leaders deal with hundreds of competing priorities at any given moment, so they rarely find time to bring employee issues to the top of the agenda. To find ways to make time and support actual listening that leads to change in ways that honor employee voice, consider the following strategies:

Team Meetings

Meetings are a necessary part of any organization. Many employees believe they are a waste of time, often because they are primarily used as vehicles for sharing information from the top. Unbeknownst to many managers, this way of sharing information can often be received as disrespectful because employees feel they are being talked at, not with. Some might suggest this information "could have been shared via email" and stop listening to the information. Rather than making these meetings feel frustrating and reinforcing a top-down flow of information that ignores employee voice, get creative and find ways to pull information from the employees.

For example, ask employees to weigh in on the agenda *before* the meeting and see if there's anything they want to add or modify; ask employees doing great work to present what they are doing to the rest of the team; let the team come up with fun icebreakers or games to build community; generate a hypothetical, thorny organizational problem and ask your team to brainstorm some answers. Consider adding morning "huddles" that include fast-paced information exchange and help build group cohesion. Try out various discussion protocols that provide the infrastructure for organic and productive conversations among employees. In other words, make it a two-way flow of information (rather than just top-down) and your team members will feel valued and more invested in being present for these meetings and beyond.

Those with larger teams in major cities and at the state level have more recently been using technology to support employee voice in regular meetings. These groups invite their entire staff to attend meetings using an online platform. Then leaders share information in small chunks of about 10 minutes each. (The brain starts to shut down, wander, or get annoyed after 10 minutes.) After each chunk, the tech person clicks the button to break up the large group into subgroups of about five employees at a time for 5-10 minutes. Employees then have a chance to discuss the information that was just presented with each other. This gives staff an opportunity to share their thinking, explore new ideas and bond with other members of the team. Once everyone returns to the large group, members of each small group share out the highlights from their conversations. The share outs can occur either out loud if the group is small enough, or in the chat if it's a very large group.

These small steps help ensure employees feel their voices are being heard and create a deeper sense of trust and belonging on the team. It also has the bonus element of significantly increasing the likelihood that the information you are sharing is heard, valued, and remembered.

Surveys

Most government organizations survey their employees every now and then, and take time to critically think and consider the results. Unfortunately, it typically ends at that point because no one at the senior level has the time, resources, or authority to make big shifts based solely on the ideas and concerns of employees. And that's where employee voice too often goes to die.

Instead of letting this happen, release or hire a few "movers and shakers" who know how to lead change efforts. Ensure they have the capacity to focus at least 80% of their time working within the institution to create and/or test out—and communicate—changes in organizational practices based on what is learned from the survey. We recommend 80% FTE because any less means the individuals responsible may get pulled off-task when other urgent matters not related to employee needs surface.

Town Halls

These venues are conducive for enabling leaders to get face time with employees, but if they are only about information sharing and a short Q&A, the event won't go far in building trust. To give these opportunities real teeth, use an effective discussion protocol or hire a seasoned facilitator to ask employees their honest opinions on what's working and what's not working within the organization. And don't stop there! Engage them in a process of brainstorming solutions to some of the toughest problems. Believe it or not, the biggest naysayers will turn into supporters if you give them ten minutes to think through ways of solving issues and an authentic platform to discuss their ideas. Use some of the ideas, and don't forget to give credit to those who helped you see something in a new light!

Mentoring

Mentoring is gaining more footing in many government spaces. Unfortunately, the recruitment and selection process is often lacking in these programs. The mentees who make it in are often the ones who are confident enough to apply, and hungry enough to know they want to get ahead in the organization. Consider nominations and developing rubrics of selection that focus efforts on finding mentees across the organization who are doing impressive work, but are more reserved, less confident, and/or from more marginalized communities. These individuals will likely become superstars who can move mountains with a little support from a mentor, but will also bring a disposition that is more amenable to Human-Centered Leadership (because they understand the power of voices that don't get heard as often).

Designing Systems to Support more Choice and Voice

Human-Centered Professional Development for Managers

A lot of organizations spend time investing in the training of their employees. An admirable approach! Yet many of these trainings reinforce the traditional "Command and Control" method of leadership. Someone makes a mistake? Write them up! Another division causing headaches? Cut them out! This reinforces all the problems outlined earlier in this chapter. To address this issue, look for specific organizations and consultants that offer workshops and coaching in ways that support the NEW kind of power—Human-Centered Leadership. Or, if your organization has the appetite and capacity, develop in-house Human-Centered Leadership courses.

These types of support have a slightly different bend than "nuts and bolts" trainings that focus exclusively on getting the job done. They tend to focus on helping managers become good at managing people instead of deliverables. For example, look for and offer professional development that helps your managers: give feedback in ways that are empowering (instead of demeaning); create psychologically safe spaces (discussed in Chapter 3); deal with conflict effectively; and lift up the voices of those under them instead of cutting them down.

The NYC Department of Education (DOE), one of the largest city government agencies in the U.S., has been turning the tide on culture by engaging in a comprehensive effort including nearly all of the strategies described above... and then some. Over the past several years, Yvonne Soto and her team at the DOE's Office of Organizational Development, Talent, and Culture have been initiating employee town halls, mentoring programs, engagement surveys, Human-Centered Professional Development for managers, cross-division networking/wellness events, and a lot more. Given the long-term nature of organizational change, it's still early in the process. However, they have recorded big improvements such as increased productivity, collaboration, and innovation across the institution.

In particular, they are seeing a shift in management style which is leading to better results for teams. For example, Matt Torell is the head of an office in charge of some of the DOE's financial operations. He has participated in many of the offerings from Yvonne's office. As a result, Matt says he went from being a "Command and Control"-style manager who struggled with empathy, and thus focused on data and outcomes, to a full-on "Engage and Inspire" manager. He felt bolstered by the new tools he developed in his Human-Centered Leadership courses and emboldened by the organization's emphasis on culture shift. This gave him the skills and confidence he needed to change the way he leads his team.

He says there were a number of things he started doing that he hadn't even thought of doing before. He engaged in one-on-one relationship-building conversations with each of his direct-reports, facilitated daily huddles, used Dotmocracy to do collective goal-setting and task-allocation with his team, and even designed an amazing "Weekly Employee Check-In Protocol." The check-in protocol supports an effective 360-degree feedback process that helps him keep his finger on the pulse of what's happening on his team while building enormous levels of trust with his team members.

In sum, Matt created structures that enabled him to listen and learn from his employees, rather than just telling them what to do at all times. As a result, he saw a huge Return on Investment (ROI). His team started collaborating better, becoming more excited about the work, and innovating. The team reports an average of 75% increase in productivity (volume of work), efficiency (working smarter, not harder), and nimbleness (ability to solve problems quickly and creatively). This provided a cost-savings of over a quarter million dollars for the team and the institution (when calculating the decrease in absenteeism and increase in productivity).

While there is still a long way to go, thanks to the intensive efforts of Yvonne and her team, Matt's Human-Centered approach to leadership is now becoming a much more common practice across the DOE, and it's even spreading beyond.

Yvonne and DOE leadership presented their powerful story of culture shift at a national education conference for school superintendents. At the end, a school district superintendent from the Midwest in the audience was overheard saying passionately to his team: "Well jeez, if they can do it in NYC, we can do it here!" He wasn't the only one thinking it. In the weeks following the presentation, at least seven large urban school systems across the nation initiated calls to Yvonne's team to learn how they could implement similar culture-building strategies in their own system.

In that space of a single 90-minute presentation, Yvonne's small team of changemakers shared their knowledge about how to build trust across a complex government structure. And in doing so, they unknowingly sparked a small movement and shifted the narrative on leadership. As Margaret Mead so aptly put it, "Never doubt that a small group of thoughtful, committed citizens can change the world; indeed, it is the only thing that ever has."

Let's wrap it up...

"Command and Control" style leadership is a traditional factory-based approach that worked for a while. It deserves credit for setting up many of our institutions and enabling systems that ensured government policy went quickly from idea to implementation.

However, in recent years, we've learned that this well-established approach is drastically inhibiting our government institutions from realizing their goals and is creating a swirl of problems and unnecessary drama that harm people and policy. From deep employee disengagement and micro-sabotage to turf wars, backstabbing, and favoritism, there are deep problems within the culture of our institutions, and very few people are talking about it. Instead, we're just manufacturing more and more policy, and scratching our heads about why we aren't seeing bigger positive change.

The good news is, you can join the many leaders within government who are changing the game by using the new methodology of "Engage and Inspire." These bold leaders invoke strategies that focus on giving employees choice and voice at all levels, and on changing institutional practices based on what is heard. Instead of information only flowing downstream, they are reversing the flow of information towards bottom-up and across. Instead of perpetuating a "tear-down" culture that belittles employees, they are promoting a "build-up" culture that empowers them.

This approach takes more time upfront to focus on listening and learning from employees at all levels of the organization—especially the front lines (because they are the closest to the users of the organizational services). But that time spent has a powerful ROI in terms of producing higher quality work, more efficiency, easier collaboration, more innovation, better talent retention, and a boost to the bottom line. The shift isn't that hard to achieve or that expensive to accomplish. All it requires is a commitment to center the ideas and feelings of all the humans who work within the organization.

Reflective questions for team discussion

This section is designed for teams or groups of people within an organization who want to debrief the chapter and/or explore avenues of thinking that could lead towards positive change.

Pre-Reflection Prompt for Team-Building

What TV shows did you binge-watch during the pandemic? (If you don't watch TV, what books did you read?)

Chapter Reflections

1. To what extent is there an atmosphere of trust and mutual support in our organization?
2. What are we doing right now that creates an "Engage and Inspire" environment?
3. Does the "Command and Control" style of leadership exist anywhere in the organization? If so, (without naming names) how does it present itself? What could be some negative repercussions of that approach?
4. Which of the Human-Centered Leadership strategies described in this chapter seem like they would have the most positive influence on the culture of our organization? Are there any strategies not mentioned that could be helpful?
5. Which Human-Centered Leadership strategies seem easiest to implement immediately?
6. What will each of us do to promote more choice and voice for the employees on our own teams?
7. What can we do (big or small) to support movement towards a more "Engage and Inspire" approach across the whole organization?

For those who would like more information and resources on how to implement the Human-Centered strategies or ideas discussed in this chapter, go to <u>centerfortransformingculture.com/resources</u>.

Chapter Two
Building the Infrastructure for Innovation
(Through Human-Centered Design)

Let's set the stage...

A small city in the Northwest is struggling financially. They are short on budget and facing major issues with their sewage system. Their mayor has the idea to address the problem by revitalizing their downtown. He negotiates a deal with an out-of-town developer who contracts to build expensive condos which will cost hundreds of millions of dollars. "Booyah!" he thinks. The influx of cash will dramatically help their budget issues. Plus, it will provide great PR for the city. He calls a press conference, declares the contract is signed, and announces the date for the grand opening ceremony of the condos.

The date of the ceremony creates an unreasonable project timeline. The Buildings Department will need to push through all the protocols in about half the time it normally would take. The mayor has confidence in his people and insists they can and will finish the project on time.

The director of the Buildings Department learns of the project from the 11 o'clock news and, surprised by the report, a sense of fear and dread washes over him. He calls the mayor to confirm the date. Instead of telling the mayor of his doubts, he tells his leadership team to drop what they are doing and put together an expedited process to enable this project to succeed. The team rallies and figures out a way to fast track all of the processes, including engaging the community, reviewing the plans for construction, and issuing permits. To reach the deadline, they put other projects on hold and reallocate resources away from current initiatives.

As the project goes full steam ahead, members of the staff feel overtaxed but continue to muscle through to achieve the mayor's ambitious deadline. The project managers feel rushed, which makes them less careful than they would otherwise be. The program associate is confused by how to file the paperwork in the new expedited processes, but finds workarounds to get the computer to accept the information. The community engagement efforts are chaotic but at least they can check the box that they did it.

At one point, one of the assistant plan reviewers notices that the developer used several structural shortcuts to save time and money. She discusses this with the deputy director but is told harshly they do not have the time to solve every minor issue with the developer. He emphasizes that their priority is the mayor's deadline. The assistant believes the shortcuts could create a serious engineering flaw, but doesn't want to be responsible for messing up the mayor's timeline and upsetting her boss. She remains quiet.

One week before the condo opening ceremony, the top three floors collapse. The buildings will require a complete overhaul of design and construction. Millions of dollars have been wasted. Multiple lawsuits are brought by suppliers who have not been paid. The mayor decides to shut the entire project down. When the press asks for comment, he tells them, "Obviously building downtown didn't work, so we're going to switch our focus and deal with our budget deficit by boosting tourism! Let me tell you about our exciting new plans..."

While this particular story was fabricated to make the point, a city planner in a major urban city admitted that "this stuff happens all the time." Other situations may not be as dramatic as the episode we just presented, but the way in which government initiatives roll out from the top can often be chaotic, ineffective, and extremely expensive for the institution and the community.

Let's unpack the problem...

The name for this type of top-down style of initiative rollout is called the "Spray and Pray" method. This refers to the idea that policy initiatives are thought up in an office somewhere in the upper echelons of management. Those ideas are subsequently sprayed across the rest of the system. Sometimes these efforts are successful and create meaningful positive change. Sometimes they don't.

Building the Infrastructure for Innovation
(Through Human-Centered Design)

What is the difference between initiatives that foster genuine positive transformation and those that don't? No one knows! That's where the prayer part comes in.

Leaving significant policy ideas up to chance is NOT the most efficient way of doing business in government institutions. There are more effective ways of instituting change that virtually guarantee success without involving a wing and a prayer. Sadly, there are mammoth issues keeping our institutions from comprehending the problem in the first place. We must tackle them before having a shot at ending the reign of "Spray and Pray."

There are three root causes keeping "Spray and Pray" alive.

Policy Implementation Isn't Sexy!

Coming up with grandiose ideas and being able to implement large-scale change by telling the rest of the system what to do is alluring. It is the essence of power. But "getting into the weeds" by actually having to spend energy engaging in the hard work of change (dealing with the pushback, the scheduling snafus, the training logistics, the errors along the way) is the opposite of feeling sexy. That feels like a headache. Most policy makers and those in senior positions tend to avoid these elements. The nitty gritty is left for the middle managers and other underlings to figure out. As a result, leaders are often out of the loop on critical information about implementation that could be taking their ideas and the success of their initiatives off-track.

Gatekeepers Are Great at Their Job

Middle managers are often considered the 'secret sauce' of any institution. They are the artists that have the challenging but noble responsibility of working out all the intricate details of leadership's initiatives so that those on the front-lines can be successful in implementing them. These are generally very intelligent and politically savvy people. Yet, those who are in "Command and Control"-style environments (as described in Chapter 1), also have the role of keeping the implementation details to a minimum. Leaders in these climates claim to be too "busy" to get into the weeds. They definitely are not interested in hearing about failure. Therefore, these middle managers become de facto gatekeepers, keeping critical information about initiative success (or lack thereof) from floating to the top. This means folks at the top are not aware of what's happening at the bottom. That creates an information juggernaut that decreases any policy's chance of success and comes with a side dish of other major problems for the organization. See the devastating consequences of "Spray and Pray" below.

Fixed Mindset & the Pendulum Swing

A huge hurdle to effective policy making is what brain science geeks like me call a "Fixed Mindset." This is the term to describe binary thinking, where a policy is seen as either effective or ineffective. It's either a success or it failed. The reality is, of course, more nuanced. Some elements of any new initiative will usually work well in some places and not as well in others.

Policy makers don't have the time or capacity for the nuances of initiative rollout because they aspire to headlines in the media that they succeeded during their time in office so they can be re-elected. This means that initiatives with strong potential to succeed but don't succeed quickly lose their shiny-new-thing appeal and end up on the chopping block. Policy leaders then assume the initiative didn't work, and move on to the next "brilliant" idea. Folks in government call this the pendulum effect. Back and forth, the pendulum swings from idea to idea with little overall transformation. Great concepts that would have worked well with more time and attention get buried and eventually forgotten.

The Devastating Consequences of "Spray and Pray" Environments

The negative consequences of "Spray and Pray" initiative rollout can be felt in many aspects of any organization. Here are some of the biggest issues that emerge.

The House is On Fire

There is a mentality in "Spray and Pray" environments that those at the most senior layers can control all the pieces that go into implementation of a new policy or change effort. The more chaos there is during transitions, the more desire to control the situation. Yet change and chaos go hand and hand. No matter how many rules and regulations one puts into effect, there will always be miscalculations, unforeseen challenges, and unanticipated questions that surface as great ideas move from theory to action. This is the nature of transformation.

This means that urgent matters (metaphorical "fires") will pop up at all hours of the day which require immediate attention. If a fire is not put out quickly, initiatives are at risk for being burnt to the ground. This puts organizational leaders in a constant state of survivalist thinking (fight or flight mode) since they are reacting to dozens of perceived threats on a daily basis. This creates a constant flow of panic energy across the institution and fosters a frenzied atmosphere with unnecessary and damaging side effects.

One example of this is the "last minute request" phenomenon. In some agencies, politicians and leaders pellet their staff and middle managers with an unending onslaught of "URGENT! HIGH PRIORITY" requests for information that needs to be answered "IMMEDIATELY!!"

Sarah, from a U.S.-sponsored office in a foreign country dealing with health networks, expresses that she gets the same message at least a few times a week. "Your office is going to do this thing, and it needs to be done tomorrow!!! They don't think about the capacity it takes to do it."

Tamara, a high-ranking middle manager in a large urban city, reports: "My team is always stressed because the leader... is always asking 20,000 questions and needs it immediately. The expectation is always to stop whatever you are doing, to do it now!"

The sense of panic around these requests forces many middle managers to abandon their post to answer leadership questions, which takes them away from the crucial work they are performing.

Chuck is a deputy director working for a senior state leader in a major U.S. city. He talks about coming into the office and wondering: "What's the fire drill for today? The mayor wants this, or the city council wants that. There were many days where I had my to-do list for the day and I didn't touch a single thing on it, because I was dealing with this request or directive."

The irony of these interruptions is that the questions are usually completely unrelated to what the organization's strategy is. Sondra, a "mover and shaker" for an agency working on housing for underprivileged communities puts it this way:

> *"We'll be moving forward with our plans, pushing to get it done in the timeline they gave us, and then we'll get this request from the leaders asking about how many apples our front-line staff have eaten that week. And then we have to rally all the troops to go find out how many apples everyone ate. It's like, who cares about the apples?! But we have to spend our time answering the question 'cause that's what they expect!"*

She's being facetious about the apples, but her point is important. The questions from higher-ups are often completely disconnected from the work being done on the ground. Because of the nature of "Spray and Pray," senior officials often don't have a good grasp on what's happening on the ground. To feel better informed, a natural reaction is to ask several questions and make requests from the staff. Unfortunately, those questions and requests often feel as if leaders are making it rain with irrelevant time-sucking inquiries that pull critical resources away from being able to solve the problem on the ground. This not only reduces the time spent on solving the problems, it also frustrates everyone caught up in the unnecessary panic energy.

There is an additional invisible harm. So many senior managers of large teams are getting pulled aside to work on these "HIGH PRIORITY" requests that managers are not able to engage in their most important job—managing!

Josephina is a lower-level manager in an employment office in the Southwest. This is what she has observed:

> *"It's been hard to find an office where manager calendars aren't inundated with meetings... and that causes absentee management. It makes employees feel less cared for, which reduces trust. It doesn't give each other visibility to each other's work."*

One of Josephina's managers actually reinforced the sentiment, saying: "As a manager, I can say if you are in charge of people, the amount of work you have and the time pressure limits your ability to connect with your team."

As a result, many employees are left to figure out things on their own, without proper oversight or support. This leads to a myriad of blunders, inefficiencies, and a less than stellar culture.

Unrealistic Timelines for Humans

There is sometimes an assumption at the top of an organization that when people below aren't implementing a new initiative fast enough, it's because they are lazy or not working hard enough. Perhaps this is true in some cases. In the larger share of cases, the reverse is true. People at the most senior layers simply underestimate how much time is necessary for a group of humans to create meaningful change. And/or, if they are elected officials, they don't have the luxury of time before the next election to incorporate timelines that are realistic for most humans.

Mitchell is a middle manager in an agency focusing on renewable energy. He expresses his frustration below:

"They tell us to be creative <around these timeframes>, but we're not trying to be stone-wallers. We're saying we've been here, and we know how long it takes to roll things like this out. It's short-sighted, and a bit disrespectful to suggest that, if we say the timeline is unrealistic, we just aren't trying hard enough."

Many leaders are so busy dealing with their own project issues that they forget or don't account for the actual time most human brains need to shift their neural pathways to alter a habit.

Think of it this way. You are a runner in a maze who has been running for five years. Every day you run on the same path, in the same direction, to the same destination point. You know the path so well that you can go super-fast without thinking. Perhaps you even brag to your friends that you can run the maze blind. Suddenly, someone changes where you need to end up in the maze. An entirely different finish line.

This forces you to start looking at new pathways. It would be ridiculous to try and run at the same fast speed while figuring out the new pattern. Your brain can't work that quickly. You need to stop and reorient yourself first. Then you will probably walk slowly through the many different paths so you can study the new patterns. You will likely make several wrong turns until you find the right corridors to your new destination point. Additionally, you must memorize the track you took, requiring you to walk it over and over and over until it becomes a new habit.

This is how one's brain executes behavior when asked to learn something new. Each new learning takes time, effort, and motivation to get over the hump of prior habit. Asking front-line workers to pivot from old habits at lightning speed is about as practical as asking them run a new maze blind.

Short-Term Gains Mask Longer-Term Problems

Some leaders get frustrated with the slow pace of change so they resort to doing what they've seen done in their own professional contexts from the past. In some cases that means writing people up, dressing employees down in front of peers, yelling, or using other fear tactics to try and get employees to change patterns quickly. This may achieve short-term results, but is woefully ineffective for the long-term. Even if people are keen to create the change being asked, our brains' neural pathways are stronger and more resilient than our desire to create the change—even when threats are calculated in.

For example, let's look at a simple change of habit outside the workplace.

My partner used to yell at me for leaving my socks on the floor at night. I WANTED to develop the habit of picking them up—both to make her happy and get her to stop yelling at me.

The fear of her yelling again gave me the impetus to change my behavior for a little while. In those weeks, the floor would be sockless and the house would be quiet.

Once my brain settled down, believing the threat was no longer there, my neural pathways would reset to the original, easier, faster pathway. I'd then revert to the old habit of leaving my socks on the floor. Even though I wanted to change my ways, my neural pathways won the day. A few weeks later, the socks would build up. She'd yell at me and we'd start the process all over again.

After many of these episodes, we figured out that yelling at me was not an effective strategy for changing my behavior. Instead, we used a team effort. I did my part—I put a post-it on the mirror that said "socks" to remind me to check if my socks were off the floor every time I brushed my teeth. And she supported the process by giving me positive reinforcement, offering a high five or a kiss every day I successfully picked up my socks for a month. (28 days is considered a standard for how long it takes to change a habit.) Eventually, I didn't need post-it notes or the positive reinforcements. I became accustomed to the new behavior! Our problem was solved.

Believing that you can engage in any change initiative without giving sufficient time *and* support for people to alter their habits of mind is under-informed, and will likely lead to ineffective implementation and poor results over the long term.

Ignoring the Broken Pieces

When you put people under extreme time-stress, managers and employees have less time to make sure the new system is running smoothly. Instead, they tend to underestimate or ignore faulty elements of the system. They often just hope and pray that the errors somehow fix themselves. Oftentimes, their prayers do not result in the desired change.

During the COVID crisis, Bethany, who is an attorney, worked on behalf of a government agency in a suburb of a major coastal city. (Heads up: when Bethany is annoyed, she doesn't hesitate to use her potty mouth to express her irritation.) This is her take on describing a policy and practice shift in her organization that the leaders tried to enact during the pandemic.

> *"They trained a bunch of people on how to do things. They did a half-ass job on training. So people mess $#!+ up. So then we get emails saying 'quit messing $#!+ up,' and you're like 'hey, whose fault is that? Bad training!'"*

Bethany, a graduate of an Ivy League institution, continues talking about her experience with the materials that came from the training.

> *"You would read those [materials], and you'd be like, 'I don't even know what you are saying to do.' Like it didn't make any sense. So, you'd write back and you'd say, 'could you please explain this?' And they're like, 'it was said in the training.'"*

Because the leaders were moving so fast, there wasn't time to consider the employee perspectives to ensure that the materials and training were having the intended effect. The training and materials got shipped out before they were ready and people like Bethany ended up getting frustrated, having insufficient information to move forward effectively. Bethany suggests that as a result, a ton of mistakes were made and a fair amount of employees struggling with COVID were not able to receive the services they needed.

Not every situation will be as dire or as urgent as COVID. But this practice happens many times in several government institutions. People at the top are running so fast that the people at the bottom feel confused, disconnected, and unsure of what exactly is being asked of them—or why.

Mental Health Tumbles

The "Spray and Pray" approach not only leads to panic energy and mismanagement (the foundation for a bevy of mistakes that can take policies off-track), but causes many employees to fall apart mentally when faced with the impossible tasks put upon them.

Here's Rebecca from a government office in a large urban city talking about her experience seeing her friend become catatonic:

> *"I saw an employee of mine freeze once. Like, couldn't move—because of the way she was admonished for making a mistake when she was moving too fast. It's hard to see a grown person, who is smart and super capable, just freeze like that. It makes you wonder... what the stress can do to some people."*

Denesia, working in a government training agency in a city in the Midwest, reinforces this with her two cents:

> *"These last-minute requests, and the expectation that everything sent upstairs is perfect... it's stressing out my team so much, and they have too much on their plate already... sometimes I worry someone is going to have a nervous breakdown."*

Speaking of, remember Bethany from earlier? She had to take six months off of work for mental health leave. Her therapist diagnosed her with PTSD (Post-Traumatic Stress Disorder) from being unable to meet the unrealistic expectations of her superiors.

Hot Head Attitudes

The irony of this behavior is that many leaders of "Spray and Pray" environments assume a cocky attitude. It's said "if you can't take the heat, get out of the kitchen." These types of remarks are meant to justify the constant state of being in many government offices where raised tempers and voices are the norm. Yet, we're seeing over and over that this "heat" is leading to countless mistakes, inefficiencies, and other dysfunctional relationships that all unequivocally lead to worse policy implementation. It doesn't take a fancy degree to recognize that there's no way human beings can learn how to implement and support positive, sustainable change if everyone is constantly in chaos mode. Perhaps the time has come to reconsider the idiom. Instead of "if you can't take the heat, get out of the kitchen," a more apt metaphor might be "if the kitchen is always on fire, you'll never learn how to cook."

There is definitely a feeling like fire and brimstone in this chapter right now. But have no fear. Luckily, this is a solvable problem! All it takes is a renewed commitment to research and development (R&D), an understanding of Human-Centered Design, and a shift in mindset for how innovation can be achieved. Keep reading to get your dose of hope and possibility.

Trends in R&D

Before we go into the potential solutions to address issues raised earlier in the chapter, it's important to point out some trends. Over the past decade, the U.S. government has been steadily reducing the amount of funds invested into Research and Development. One study suggests it has slid so low, the figures are now about the same levels as the 1950s.[10] The study also offers "there should be no question that this has resulted in stagnant productivity growth, lagging competitiveness, and reduced innovation." There's even a running joke in many leadership circles: "government innovation is an oxymoron."

Some have argued that the reason for this trend is political. It's easier to get elected focusing on ideology and blaming the "other side" for problems than to come up with new, creative, and actionable answers to those problems. Creating new solutions is difficult, but government agencies that use the "Spray and Pray" method of implementation find it practically impossible. Ergo, politicians lose incentive to focus on improving the system.

Corporations, though, have been steadily increasing how much they invest in R&D. There is a clear understanding in the corporate landscape that innovation supports their competitive edge. We've seen incredible advancements in the private sector that have shaped our world, from self-driving cars to watches that can track our health. The most successful of these companies are using something called "Human-Centered Design" to help them achieve these powerful new levels of success. A small smattering of these companies include: Spotify, Fitbit, Venmo, Toyota, Nike, IKEA, Apple, Microsoft, and Google.

By design, private sector investments focus first on increasing profit. Sure, there are some societal gains, but these are often a welcome byproduct, and not the main dish. This limits our current infrastructure and capacity for coming up with new solutions to real global issues. This makes it less likely that government will be able to solve critical issues like climate change, food insecurity, and violent conflict.

There are pockets of individuals within many government agencies actively seeking new innovative solutions, but these small teams are often woefully underfunded and/or have a hard time gaining traction—especially if those innovations could possibly be seen as jeopardizing revenue for major corporate industries. As a result, the U.S. and much of our world have been crawling at a snail's pace on innovation, while corporations have been blowing it out of the sky (literally, if you include Virgin Airlines founder Richard Branson sending the first airplane into space).

The gap has become so wide that many government agencies now "farm out" innovation. They bring in highly paid consultants and corporate firms to do research and offer intricate and expensive reports making recommendations to support improvement. Yet too often, these reports end up on someone's shelf collecting dust and rarely translate into wide-scale meaningful change.

The interesting part is that government agencies have the power and the capacity to lead the charge on innovation. All they need is a better understanding of Human-Centered Design and the willingness to draw on the talents and passion of the people that work there.

Let's solve this together...

Human-Centered Design is a cutting-edge new process of product/service development being used in many corporate and some government workplaces. It's also called User-Centered Design, Continuous Improvement, Design Thinking, Improvement Science, Hacking, and there's probably a few new ones that were created in the weeks since this book has been published. I'll continue to utilize the term Human-Centered Design, but feel free to replace the language you are familiar with in your head if that is more comfortable.

The trend is catching on at high speed. There is an explosion of companies developing models for integrating Human-Centered Design. Some of these include IDEO's Design Thinking method, the Carnegie Foundation's Networked Improvement Communities, the Office of Personnel Management's Innovation Lab and my own... the Center for Transforming Culture's Kaleidoscope Method.

Each of these models has their own approach and flavor. What they have in common is that they all bring together groups of employees from all levels of the organization to engage in the art of change. These groups typically use a structured process using trial and error to identify creative, sustainable solutions to tough organizational problems. This strategy is different from most reforms because the focus is not on the *content* of reform, but on the *process* of reform. It is literally changing the way institutions are thinking about change.

For example, rather than seeing products, policy or services as "finished" projects, institutions using Human-Centered Design use a growth mindset—seeing each product and service as a work in progress. Instead of believing an initiative either "worked" or "didn't work," they take a more nuanced perspective. They understand that any given initiative is going to work well in some places, and not so well in other places. Rather than ending funding for initiatives that don't work everywhere after the first crack, they focus on digging in to see where it's working well, engage in real-time research to understand why it's successful in those spaces, and then invest time and funding into expanding the conditions for success to more spaces. This is an ongoing process that celebrates progress, not perfection.

This process does take more time, and it does not produce the adrenaline rush of an instant headline claiming victory in the papers. However, it does lead to slow and steady improvement in practices and policies that achieve a powerful positive cumulative effect over time.

Anyone can implement Human-Centered Design in their workplace. All it takes is bringing together employees in small teams and a commitment to the core principles. The principles may have a different flavor based on whose model you are reviewing, but here are some that I've found to be the most critical to success.

1. From Top-Down Feedback to Bottom-Up and Across

Instead of sending ideas for implementation downstream from the top, successful Human-Centered Leaders create regular intentional processes to communicate with those responsible for implementation of the change effort. Feedback from these communities is imperative to learn where the program is flowing well and where the system is breaking down.

These data points are quickly brought to the attention of leaders, middle managers and front-line workers. Everyone involved is aware of what changes are necessary for a smooth transition. This information sharing enables funding to be used more efficiently, drastically reduces unnecessary questions that pull critical personnel off-task, and creates a pathway for rapid improvement of current and future initiatives.

For example, Gaby Hurtado is the Medical Countermeasures Coordinator and Manager of the Vaccination Rollout at the City of Long Beach Health and Human Services Department in California. After every health intervention, Gaby facilitates a robust protocol for engaging in rapid information sharing that flows bottom-up, across, and top-down. The protocol enables front-line workers from doctors and nurses to volunteers to always have an opportunity to weigh in on what worked, what didn't, and offer suggestions for what needs to change.

That information is aggregated and sent to Gaby, who looks at the data to ascertain patterns. She then works with cross-functional teams at more senior levels to co-create potential solutions to address any inefficiency in the process. That cross-functional team looks at the root causes of the kinks, solves the problems, and scales the solutions quickly and easily so it becomes seamless. Health initiative success is practically guaranteed because they make problem-hunting and fixing a part of the package every time.

A good example of where this worked was the vaccine rollouts. Most people were surprised at how smooth the process was set up when they went to get their shot. The U.S. has been mired in lots of logistical and political challenges around the pandemic, and gaining access to the vaccine has been imperfect. But the actual rolling out of hundreds of millions of doses once available felt relatively easy. Most people had good experiences, which is odd for any initiative of that size. And the numbers are compelling. In fact, the U.S. vaccine rollout is currently considered among the best in the world![11]

Gaby also uses other protocols to ensure information is flowing in all directions. One of them is the "what if" protocol. This protocol creates a platform for cross-functional teams within the institution to engage in drills based on a series of "what if" scenarios. These scenarios allow all parts of the organization to determine how the system would respond to emergency worst case situations (i.e., bioterrorism, natural disaster, nuclear fallout, etc.). This enables the institution to proactively find the problems and unintended consequences of their responses BEFORE an actual disaster strikes. Gaby then works with each of the cross-functional teams to modify their policies and practices so that everyone is on the same page and better prepared for when a catastrophe actually occurs.

As a result of this high level of preparedness, the Department is ready for almost every scenario. Plus, there is an important add-on benefit. Everyone in the organization becomes accustomed to being in improvement mode. They constantly look for possible unintended consequences of their actions, strategies to collaborate better, and ways to improve any and all practices to make the entire system work more smoothly. They are the ultimate learning culture. That makes the institution more innovative, more nimble, and more likely to succeed in good times or disastrous ones.

At the same time, employees feel more valued because they see that their input is being included in important decision-making efforts. They are literally a part of creating the solutions, and more directly helping to make communities safer. This creates a lot of positive knock-on effects for team culture like high trust, easy collaboration, and a passionate workforce that is dedicated to bringing their best selves to work every day.

One of the more poignant moments of my interview with Gaby was when I asked how her organization became so adept at systems improvement. She offered several reasons. The one I remember most vividly was: "Katrina is always in the back of our heads. It is a blot on our record, and reminds us we need to figure out ways to do better."

This comment gave me goosebumps. The disconnects, confusion, and chaos that ensued from the devastating hurricane led to deadly and traumatic outcomes for too many people. Instead of sheepishly crawling under a rug to pretend it didn't happen, the emergency preparedness community has learned from the mistakes and failures. They stepped up their game and created new systems and protocols for deep institutional learning to ensure such a misfortune would never happen again. This community now has some of the best systems in the world—and many lives are being saved because of it. This is the power of Human-Centered Design and Leadership.

2. Empathy and Connection

The first step of Human-Centered Design is to empathize with those who are most impacted by the problem. That could mean empathy for the employees implementing various policies, or for the communities being served by the policies, or both. Empathy doesn't come naturally to many government institutions. It requires an effort to research, connect with and listen to the needs, opinions, and problems faced by those in the community and everyone affected by the change.

Rather than ignoring the complaints and pain points of those engaged in the work of change, this process focuses innovators' attention on learning all about them! This learning process helps to build high-trust relationships across the organization and in communities. It also enables institutions to quickly improve the quality of their services and the community's reception of those services.

For example, let's look at Carmelyn Malalis, the Commissioner and Chair for the NYC Commission on Human Rights. When she came onboard in 2015, she revamped the community service centers in each of the city's five boroughs. These centers were established for the sole purpose of building relationships and understanding the needs of the community. So she began hiring people from the community to serve as liaisons. She ensured these liaisons had multiple language skills to connect with all members of the community in meaningful ways, and the facilitation skills to share important information in ways that were accessible.

Employees at the centers are also expected and empowered to engage the community in whatever way feels right to them, whether that's going out to lunch with religious and school leaders, hosting events for shared learning among stakeholders, or facilitating workshops that incorporate two-way listening protocols. Whatever the process, staff are expected to glean the insights from their engagements and share community concerns or ideas with Carmelyn and the leadership team. Commissioner Carmelyn Malalis then prioritizes those needs in the overall strategic plan and invites her team to identify creative ways to address them through their agency.

Building the Infrastructure for Innovation
(Through Human-Centered Design)

The commissioner believes having a better understanding of the lived experiences of community members and creating stronger connections with those in the community (in addition to their aggressive enforcement of human rights law) is what has led to the turnaround in the agency's effectiveness and reputation. Indeed, the institution has gone from being labeled as ineffective and having "no teeth" to being renowned as one of the most powerful human rights institutions in the nation. Since the transition, it's more than doubled the number of community workshops, increased the number of closed cases on human rights abuses by 216%, created 36 amendments to strengthen human rights law, and won over 20 awards and recognitions from the community and elected officials. This is one story of how the power of prioritizing empathy and connection manifests itself.

3. Try, Revise, Repeat

Many organizations using the "Spray and Pray" method tend to roll out an initiative after there has been an enormous amount of time, energy, and funding poured into making sure everything is perfect. This is an impossible standard considering nothing is ever perfect—especially the first time out.

Groups involved in Human-Centered Design spend a fair amount of time looking at the data in an effort to find root causes of problems and mitigate risks around projects. But the process leans much more on taking action rather than waiting for the exact right solution or perfect conditions for roll out! To do this effectively leaders conduct initial tests of products or initiatives on a small scale first.

Dave Codoroli, a front-line worker at the Roads Division in Marin County Public Works, believes this piece is critical to success. He says, "You gotta take baby steps, so when you slip and fall, you don't hurt your back." His metaphor illustrates that when we are slower and more intentional about each change we make, we have more control over our actions and more ability to course-correct when things aren't working.

Most of the time in Human-Centered Design is spent in this space— trying out and testing new ideas (or beta-testing) at a small scale. One of the key elements is that those trying out new ideas look for ways in which their innovative products or services do not work. That means potential for failure is acknowledged and baked into the process.

After the first fail, those involved focus their efforts on collecting data to learn what didn't work and why it didn't work, revise their projects based on the data, and then try it again, scaling up as they see more and more successes. Then they collect more data, figure out what didn't work and why, and go revise again. They repeat this trial and error process over and over, until the data show the service or product working so well, in so many different contexts, that it is sure to be successful when rolled out across the organization.

For example, Shannon Wheeler Roberts is the Chief of Communications and Operational Readiness at the Department of Homeland Security's U.S. Citizenship and Immigration Services agency. She works in the part of the agency which focuses primarily on refugees and asylum seekers. She and her team began using Human-Centered Design as a method to empower employees to improve their work experience and improve the quality of work while leading innovation strategies to address the organization's most-pressing challenges.

Her team created innovation working groups and invited staff from across the organization to join. These groups engage in all of the stages of the Human-Centered Design Process, including: identification of a problem, empathizing and researching to fully understand the issue, prototyping solutions, and piloting and revising the solutions as many times as needed to get it right.

They are still early in the process but have seen a number of micro-innovations surface. One of their innovation teams created a new process for officers to review asylum applications. Rather than assigning officers cases from any country at any time, they decided to try out a new method. They gave a small team of officers intensive training where they learned about the specific conditions of a particular country or region in an in-depth way. Then, they had those officers focus singularly on applicants from that country or region for a short period of time. The goal was to see if this training and temporary focus period would enable officers to develop a much higher level of expertise in the country, including human rights conditions, which would improve the officer's work experience as well as the quality of the adjudication.

After one pilot test, the team discovered the modified process led to an increase in officers' confidence and job satisfaction as well as the quality of their work. A big success! However, the group also discovered that officers were reporting burnout with this method from too much repetition. So rather than be satisfied with a mostly successful outcome, the team revised the process and has piloted once more. They plan to continue to build on their successes while also building in protocols that enable staff to feel more connected and engaged in teamwork throughout the process.

This is what Human-Centered Design looks like. It's not typically a valiant victory that gets headlines in the papers for changing the landscape of the country. It's usually a set of small micro-innovations led by passionate employees to make processes more efficient and more effective. The end result is that as the many micro-innovations accrue over time, policies get much better at serving communities, and employees become much more engaged and better at work.

Incidentally, sometimes micro-innovations lead to macro-innovations that do make headlines.

4. Carve Out Time for Change

At the heart of Human-Centered Design is the strategy of "trial and error." This approach is used in everything from blasting rocket ships to the moon to which shampoo to use. This is the basic principle for how institutions and humans improve. Unfortunately, the term "trial and error" is missing a key word that stumps many government agencies seeking to stoke innovation—REVISE! Trying something and figuring out why it doesn't work is half the battle. The other half is taking the time to revise the original concept/design to incorporate the learning.

Revising is dreaded because of the amount of time it requires to accomplish. Humans are reluctant to detach from their original vision. When someone puts blood, sweat, and tears into birthing a new initiative, it can feel easier to merely give up than bear the thought of spending all that time again to start from a new direction. This is a common human reaction, one that causes excellent policy efforts to get discarded, rather than revised, when they fail to show immediate results.

The most practical way to avoid this pitfall is to carve out and safe-guard time for those innovating to collect data and then redesign their projects based on the evidence. It establishes the expectation that any given project or initiative is not expected to immediately succeed; that changes are a necessary part of the process. This benefits those creating the initiative to not feel defeated when everything doesn't work perfectly on the first, second, or even third try. As a result, teams are willing to roll with the punches and keep moving forward on changing the product or service until they eventually succeed.

Here's the caveat. Just telling employees to meet and do the work of innovating on their own in their spare time doesn't cut it in fast-paced government agencies. People have great intentions to meet up and work on powerful solutions to well-entrenched institutional problems. But innovation is too often seen as a luxury add-on item, without a strong sense of urgency built in.

When an employee receives a last-minute request to support their boss, or is required to put out a "fire" in the office, or is feeling panicked that they won't get their routine everyday work done on time, they will often ignore the innovation meeting. They might want to go, but they are going to prioritize the meetings that keep them out of trouble with the higher-ups. If an innovation meeting gets postponed and it is difficult to find a new time everyone can attend, it's easy for the meeting to fall off the radar. Regrettably, if there is not a time and space carved out for this work, the effort is likely to lose momentum, get deprioritized, and quietly die out.

Therefore, it is imperative that leaders of Human-Centered Design sanction time and space to ensure participating employees are provided with what they need to succeed. Organizations can test the Google method and officially give all employees 20% time (one day a week) to focus on innovation work. Leaders can set aside bi-weekly or monthly meetings JUST for innovation work (and make known the expectation that it is a priority for all participating employees). One can use the LEAN Six Sigma approach and set aside 5-7 days to have an intense innovation retreat where all other work shuts down so all employees can attend and find ways to improve the organization. Or you can even take a team of employee innovators off-line part time to focus on nurturing the innovations.

Erica Mohr is one such leader. Erica was a commander in the Coast Guard responsible for officer professional development. A unique challenge of the military services is that they must grow their CEO from age 18. They are not legally authorized to hire externally. This means robust officer development programs are essential. Erica was assigned as part of an intentionally diverse innovation team, representing all stakeholder groups, to develop a course for midgrade officers to support their transition from subject matter experts (ship drivers, inspectors, and pilots) to organizational leaders (writing policy and participating in the federal government budget process).

It was a tall order. Numerous groups over three decades had been commissioned to solve this problem. These groups had great ideas and strategies, but none had ever moved out of the recommendations stage to actually implement a course.

To try and figure out the issue, Erica's team began their work by interviewing participants of previous work teams who had recommended changes and not seen them through to implementation. It quickly became clear to Erica that what no team had done before was clear their plates to make the implementation a priority. Everyone was so overwhelmed, that it was easier to assume someone else, with more time, was going to do the actual work.

So she made the case to her boss, asking for time off for her and the team to get this right. She convinced him to give her six months off regular job duties and take many things off the plates of her innovation team so they could focus on thinking outside the box and execute a live 10-month pilot.

The strategy worked. Her boss gave her and the team the time they needed. Her team was then able to focus their energy on deep innovative work, rather than trying to juggle the efforts with full-time loads. This time gave them the flexibility they needed to implement a 10-month prototype, seeking constant feedback from 30 participants.

Rather than spending a year designing a perfect product "at the white board," the group instead enlisted the help of 30 beta test students who were immersed in the program and provided a constant feedback loop to help them iterate and improve upon their original concept. Erica even earned the nickname of "delta" from her regular feedback sessions with participants asking: what's working (+) and what can we do better (Δ).

The final product has continued to evolve over the years and is considered a huge success. The course is now mandatory for midgrade officers and has made a measurable difference in many lives, as officers feel more prepared for the organizational challenges of leadership.

5. Process to Scale

One of the reasons Human-Centered Design is so effective is because the people responsible for implementing the new solutions feel ownership in making it successful. The solutions are partially based on their ideas, making them more invested in ensuring all of the elements of implementation are addressed with thoughtfulness and gusto. This creates a cadre of inspired leaders on the front lines who have the knowledge, the grit, and the passion to ensure that the project will work—no matter what it takes.

Here's the rub. Let's say a small group of people in one division of your agency are initiating a Human-Centered Design process and come up with a mind-blowing solution which the data indicates will fix an age-old systemic problem. Let's say it works so well that the agency wants to scale the solution to other parts of the institution. This is great news for the original group! But the agency runs the risk of replicating the same problem as "Spray and Pray." If employees who were not a part of the Human-Centered Design team are being told they must implement the new solution, they may still get the same feeling as if it is being ordered by senior management. They had no input into it.

Building the Infrastructure for Innovation
(Through Human-Centered Design)

Organizations can address this issue by asking each group expected to implement the newly designed solution to make at least one change that makes it their own. The change can be nominal (perhaps they change the name of the solution for their context) or substantive (perhaps they design new tools or tweak the solution to have a different focus). The type of change is less important than getting the ownership and enthusiasm of those doing the work.

Do you risk ruining the solution by allowing groups to change it at will? That's a possibility. But the glory of Human-Centered Design is that there are always opportunities to course-correct. So if a change doesn't work, the group can continue modifying the solution until it succeeds. Plus, Human-Centered Leaders put their money on the belief that giving people the power and support to try out their own solutions will always turn out better than demanding they implement something they don't believe in and don't care about.

Let's wrap it up...

"Spray and Pray" methodology is a chancy way of doing business in government structures. Yet a number of government agencies continue to roll the dice. They come up with brilliant ideas for how to change the system to be more effective, put tons of resources into perfecting the plan, and watch as their fabulous ideas get swallowed by the black hole of implementation pitfalls: unrealistic timelines, insufficient capacity, distractions from the project, and unwillingness to hear about or address challenges. The result is that billions of dollars get wasted on initiatives that had tremendous potential but fell short of creating the desired change immediately. This process not only wastes taxpayer money, it also frustrates those policy makers who wanted to see their ideas come to fruition. It creates a lot of distrust among employees and makes systemic improvement of government feel impossible.

Fortunately, there are a myriad of government agencies who have figured out how to address this problem using the principles of Human-Centered Design. Rather than coming up with the perfect solution for a problem at the top and sending it down the pike to be implemented, they encourage people at all levels of the organization to constantly test out new solutions. Rather than broad-sweeping initiatives that are difficult for employees to absorb, they create micro-innovations that employees feel deep ownership of and are excited to champion through.

The primary difference is movement from a fixed to a growth mindset. Leaders would do well to learn from history and finally shelve the idea that any initiative will work the first time out of the gate. Instead, they need to embrace the idea that mistakes and failure are part of the process, and that those missteps represent the best opportunities to catapult growth!

To make it work, it does require a few changes to typical management practices. Leaders in this approach need to create space for empathy and connection to those responsible for implementing policies, including the end-user of those policies. They need to develop structures for fast-paced information sharing across all layers of the organization—from the bottom up, the top down, and laterally across. Most importantly, leaders must invest the time to let cross-functional teams of employees test out new ideas and have the flexibility to ensure great solutions get adopted.

Of course, there are additional cost implications here. Giving employees the time to design, test out, and help great innovations scale requires a shifting of resources. But if those resources mean that government institutions can save billions of taxpayer dollars by getting to success quicker and more efficiently, creating trust across the organization, and finding innovative sustainable solutions to well-entrenched global problems, doesn't that seem like a rational trade-off?

Reflective questions for team discussion

This section is designed for groups of people within an organization to discuss and explore options for initiating Human-Centered Leadership strategies.

Pre-Reflection Prompt for Team-Building

What is one thing that you haven't done in your life yet, but still hope to do in the future?

Chapter Reflections

1. Where have we seen any examples of "Spray and Pray" implementation in places that we've worked?
2. What are some of the negative repercussions we've seen from the "Spray and Pray" approach?
3. Is our organization and/or division more "Spray and Pray" or Human-Centered Design? What is your evidence (what have you seen or heard that makes you think this way)?
4. Which of the Human-Centered Design strategies described in this chapter seem like they would have the most positive influence on the implementation of new ideas in our organization? Are there any strategies not mentioned that could be helpful?
5. Which Human-Centered Design strategies feel possible to try out in our division/organization?
6. What are some things we can do to create a more Human-Centered Design approach in our division?
7. What can we do (big or small) to support movement towards a more Human-Centered Design approach across the whole organization?

For those who would like more information and resources on how to implement the Human-Centered strategies or ideas discussed in this chapter, go to <u>centerfortransformingculture.com/resources</u>.

Chapter Three
Creating a Psychologically Safe Environment

Let's set the stage...

Raymond is a recently hired computer programmer in a power plant in the Southwest who moved to town with his family for this job. Out of work since the pandemic, he is grateful for the opportunity. He is responsible for coding data that gets transferred from one unit of the plant to another. On his third week on the job, he watches Jim, one of his tech colleagues, get chewed out and threatened to be fired by their boss. This situation occurs in front of the entire team because Jim made an error that brought down the website for six hours. The berating is harsh. Raymond is so disturbed he slumps into his chair, as if to hide under the table. He feels awful seeing a member of his team get badgered and humiliated in front of the group. Everyone knows that Jim didn't make the error intentionally.

A few weeks later, Raymond realizes he made a coding mistake in the electric grid. He considers telling his boss but remembers the event with Jim. He calculates the risk. The chances of the coding error leading to anything critical are extremely small because the system is relatively stable. Certainly, his error is not worth having to face the wrath of his boss and put his job at risk since the likelihood of something going wrong is so trivial. He remains quiet.

Three months later, an unusual cold storm hits the region. Temperatures drop below freezing, which the area is not accustomed to. People start cranking up the heat at much higher levels than the plant is set up to support. This taxes the system and causes Raymond's bad coding to execute. As a result, the electrical grid goes dead for three days during some of the coldest temperatures the region has ever seen. Seventy-six people die, mostly of hypothermia.

This particular story was fabricated to explain a point. The tendency to hide mistakes and problems in the system for fear of getting "in trouble" is all too real. In government cultures with a strong punitive mindset, the vast majority of employees are too intimidated to admit to their superior when they make a mistake. As a result, mistakes similar to Raymond's get swept under the rug. This eventually causes a major amount of damage to the organization and, often, to the public.

Recently we have become more aware of the damaging effects of employees being fearful of admitting mistakes. The situation has become so dire that brain science geeks have even given it a term. It's called "psychological safety." The emergence of the term is important because it enables us to better understand how to create conditions where people at work feel safe sharing their questions, concerns, and mistakes rather than hiding them.

Unfortunately, those working in government cultures with strong top-down or "Command and Control" leadership styles often do not feel they have this option. Psychological safety in these environments is less likely because of the conditions we describe in Chapters 1 and 2. Managers are often asked to take on massive responsibilities with little to no extra support, given timelines that are woefully unrealistic, and are expected to have superhuman powers to achieve these goals in spite of these conditions. Even when these managers do manage to achieve high levels of success, they are still skewered when they make a mistake.

Here's Shital, a mid-level manager who has felt the pinch of this issue, describing her context:

> *"When you are severely understaffed, with just as big of a workload, there are going to be errors. There's just no way you can do everything, and some balls are going to get dropped. But you are only being judged on these big things. Any one mistake will wipe out the 90% of the good work your team has been doing."*

Rachel, a leader, agrees with this sentiment and offers what it does to the employees responsible for doing the work:

"We're told 'we want you to achieve these goals but in half the time and with 10% of the budget. And there's no room for mistakes.' It leads to fear, apprehension, dread, and anxiety."

Jason is a respected leader who opened up about the terrifying mantra that penetrates his government agency at the highest levels:

"You're only as good as your last mistake."

A few years ago, I conducted a small-scale study of government agencies with strong top-down leadership and found only 11% of employees felt a strong sense of psychological safety in those institutions. That means only about one out of ten employees felt psychologically safe. Two people came up to me after the study was presented and told me they thought that number was high. Ironically, I can't even report the specifics of that study out of fear that sharing the data will get people at those institutions in trouble!

A lack of psychological safety doesn't only hurt the individual employees struggling to keep up with the set of impossible standards. It also significantly hurts the institution's ability to be successful in a number of ways, as detailed below.

The Harm Done in Institutions Without Psychological Safety

Blame Games

When mistakes are made in a space that doesn't tolerate mistakes, people start behaving poorly. Rather than risk getting fired, written up, or called out in front of their peers (or worse, the public), leaders and organizations start pointing fingers at each other. The hope is that, if you accuse someone else (whether or not they are truly at fault), the blame shifts away from you and keeps you safe. This initiates a cut-throat round of the Blame Game, where accusations begin to fly and everyone tries to keep their head down to avoid the fallout.

This approach means a lot of time and energy gets spent looking for a scapegoat rather than on actually fixing the problem. As a result, root causes are not addressed, problems recur in the future, and some poor individual who was in the wrong place and at the wrong time ends up taking the heat for something that may not have been their fault.

Here's one telling example that is so awful, it's almost preposterous.

I had a colleague, John, who worked for a large urban school district in the Midwest. The district had a very strong top-down "Command and Control" culture. John had the job of deciding whether to close the schools when a bad snowstorm was predicted to hit. It's an anxiety-producing job because you can't control the circumstances, yet there are strong consequences if you make the wrong prediction. If you leave the schools open and the storm is horrific, you are called out for being reckless and endangering lives. If you close the schools and the storm is milder than predicted, you were premature and overreacted.

Every time there was a storm approaching, John would stay up all night listening to weather reports, barely leaving the room for bathroom breaks for fear of missing a possible clue about shifts in the weather. At four o'clock in the morning, he'd take the best guess he could, make the call, and cross his fingers he was right!

He had a good record of guessing correctly a few times that year. But during one storm predicted to be severe, he guessed incorrectly. He had closed the schools based on all the reports. Then the storm took an unexpected turn at the very last minute. The next morning, he and everyone in the system woke up to a beautiful sunny day, with not a single snowflake falling from the sky.

People were irate, the press had a field day, and a number of activists took this moment to shame the city. The mayor needed to deflect that bad press, so he blamed the school board, who then blamed the superintendent, who then blamed John—who was the perfect fall guy. John was then ceremoniously reamed for his incompetency in public and taken to task for all the dollars wasted and people put out by his wrong call. He was also told several times that he might get fired over this debacle, and was put on notice moving forward.

Is this as bananas to you as it is to me? A grown man gets blamed, publicly shamed, dragged in the mud, and almost fired because he wasn't a telepath and didn't have intimate knowledge of what many people would call an Act of God? Over something that is literally impossible for a human to know!? If this doesn't show the ridiculous nature of punitive-minded government systems, I don't know what else would.

Paranoia and the Conditions for Corruption

Over the past ten years in my work with government systems, I've heard the same refrain coming from leaders when I ask them if they feel safe in their job: "I feel like I'm going to get fired every single day."

This opinion is rooted in a pervasive feeling that exists in leadership circles of strong top-down environments. Everyone knows they can become the fall guy for something that is out of their control at any moment. Anyone can accuse them of incompetence at any point. This leads to paranoia and panic energy that fosters a deep distrust of those around them and negatively affects the work.

I recall one leader of a major city agency who was mentoring me and offered advice to support my trajectory in the agency. He advised me, "keep your cards close to your chest. You don't want them to know what you're thinking." He was trying to be helpful, but I was flabbergasted. How the heck are we supposed to accomplish anything of value if we can't tell people what we are actually thinking?

This state of affairs, aside from being absolutely heartbreaking, is also terrible for government business. It means that the most leaders are leading from a space of fear—often in fight or flight (or freeze and appease) mode. That means that survival mode kicks in and decisions are being based on how to keep one's job more than what is logically good for the system.

In the extreme, this survivalist thinking can lead to the conditions for corruption. People engage in cover ups to hide the truth, engage in unethical reciprocal favors to "cover one's behind," intentionally set others up for failure, and engage in other shady practices to keep themselves and the institution safe from harm.

Innovation Killer

In an atmosphere without any psychological safety, employees are afraid to share information that might lead to them being seen as doing anything incorrect. So they take the safer route and simply don't share. Instead, most employees keep their heads down and focus on their own work, keeping their thoughts and ideas to themselves. At least they know if they stay focused on what they know, chances are small that they will do anything wrong and get in trouble.

This leads to a negative condition called the "common knowledge" effect, where the dominant or most common knowledge is what everyone assumes to be true. There is no learning taking place and no questioning of assumptions. It also means that there is very little updating of information to incorporate new ideas or shifts in thinking. Everyone just assumes that what they know is true and tries to keep any individuals or any information that challenges that assumption at bay. This reinforces silos in government agencies, kills the spirit of collaboration and means that decisions are being made without all the information necessary—in other words, irresponsible decision-making.

In addition, employees, like the rest of us, know that any time we try something new, there is a learning curve. That means not being efficient at it for a while, and likely making mistakes. That's a scary proposition for employees in a psychologically unsafe environment. It's easier to merely dodge any changes being requested from on high and stick with what they know. This squashes innovation like an unwanted bug under a shoe. If people are too afraid to change, no matter how beneficial the idea, innovation will simply not occur.

Hard to Report Positive Outcomes

I worked with one school system in a major U.S. city that was focused on creating a more equitable surrounding for students. They were trying out a new strategy to address the high number of suspensions of young Black male students. It turned out to be a powerful strategy that, within a year, dropped suspension rates of this group by half. HALF! That is a mind-blowing result for any educational initiative... but especially one focused on equity, which tends to be a more slippery metric to capture.

I was friends with the person running the data and knew her to be brilliant, thorough, and extremely scientific about her number crunching. There were many other teams that corroborated the data, so their research efforts were watertight. This wasn't a case of skimming the data or fudging the numbers. This was actual, positive, and significant change. Everyone in the leadership circles knew it.

Yet the school system was reluctant to share the positive news with the media or the public. They believed that putting out any positive data or celebrating the good news would bring out the sharks. Someone who is a critic of the institution (be it a media watchdog or community group) could find some reason to discount the data and use it as leverage to expose other cracks in the system. For example, "maybe they got the suspension rates down for Black male students but look at their inadequate numbers supporting Black female students!"

It's a lose-lose situation because the public and media both have a fixed mindset which often feels like a zero-sum game. If the whole system isn't showing irrefutable massive progress, it's easier to bury good news than to share it and have to withstand the pointed arrows of those who want to ding the system.

This has a doubly negative effect because it means the public usually only gets access to part of the story in the media—the bad part. That reinforces a negative view of government, which causes these spaces to be even more psychologically unsafe.

The Benefits of Having Psychological Safety at Work

We've been talking a lot about the harms that accrue when psychological safety is not present. But let's flip the switch for a moment and talk about the powerful gains that are made when psychological safety is present and abundant.

In psychologically safe environments, team members feel secure sharing their mistakes because they know that instead of being blamed, the team will focus on discovering the root cause of the issue and solving the problem. There is no need for all of the drama that comes with Blame Game culture. This means that leaders feel less pressure to "cover their behind" and are less likely to engage in shady practices. It also means that because the root causes of problems are being addressed swiftly, the organization is improving at much faster rates than organizations lacking this process.

Team members also feel safe to take risks and innovate. They aren't scared to fail because they understand that failure is merely a stepping stone for getting to success. Without the fear of retribution, they become curious. They have the freedom to try new ways of doing things. And those experiments lead to creative, out-of-the-box thinking that drives innovative ideas forward. Some innovations are small, some are very large. Either way, innovation is happening all the time at all different levels of the organization.

As a result of employees becoming accustomed to innovating often, they are much more flexible to adapt to change. If something catastrophic like the pandemic hits, people in psychologically safe spaces are able to move quickly to pivot and implement new plans. This improves an organization's nimbleness and ensures that good decisions are being made at a fast pace.

Finally, individual employees are more likely to take the initiative to improve their work processes and become more self-sufficient, simply because they are empowered to do so.

Some Research for Your Consideration

Google did a study looking for the key characteristics of their most successful teams. Basically, they looked at all the teams who helped the institution become one of (if not the) largest, most successful, and most globally recognized technology companies on our planet. For the record, they now boast a reach of about four billion people—more than half of the Earth's population. The study's primary investigators went on the hunt to find the common attributes of the teams that were most responsible for helping Google to achieve this level of success.

You might think that advanced technical knowledge and skills in STEM (Science, Technology, Engineering, and Math) would be first on that list. After all, STEM is dominating the current narrative in school policy, state priorities, and philanthropic investments. However, STEM barely blipped on their radar. By far, the most common attribute across all the highest performing teams was psychological safety. When teams felt safe enough to take risks and make mistakes, they became the finest teams in the world.

Amy Edmonson, a prominent Harvard researcher, reinforced Google's data. Her studies showed that the highest-achieving hospital teams were always the ones with psychological safety.[11] At first, the figures are counter-intuitive, but the hospital teams that reported the *most* mistakes were the ones with the best patient outcomes. This is because those hospitals gave permission to the doctors to admit missteps and learn from them rather than try to cover them up (which increases the odds that they recur). A number of additional studies suggest other benefits from psychological safety in the healthcare industry, including improvements in: patient safety, patient experience, institutional learning, team performance, employee engagement, collaboration, and job satisfaction.[13]

Some thought-leaders are even exposing a lack of psychological safety as the root cause of some of our biggest disasters in history— including the space shuttle Challenger explosion, the financial crisis of 2008,[14] and the Chernobyl nuclear meltdown.[15] More recently, theories are springing up that a lack of psychological safety is essentially the culprit for the spread of the COVID-19 pandemic.[16]

Let's unpack the problem...

All humans make mistakes, right? "To err is human; to forgive, divine." This phrase illuminates one of the most basic and well-accepted principles of being a human. No one reading this is going to state that they and everyone on their team are perfect, or that they've successfully weeded out the possibility of ever committing errors in the future. So why do such a large number of government cultures struggle with this issue of admitting mistakes? To answer this question, we need to take a long hard look at the root causes.

(It's going to get ugly, but do not fret! We're only pointing this out so we can learn how to solve these issues, which is explained in the subsequent section).

Gotcha Journalism

People in the media tend to see themselves as truth-seekers— exposing corruption, greed, and cover-ups in the name of justice and transparency. This is a fair and noble cause. Unfortunately, some reporters and editors are unaware of their own role in actually creating the corruption they seek to expose.

There is a mantra used in traditional media: "If it bleeds, it leads." This denotes the media's tendency to focus on situations that create harm. That's because people tend to purchase papers or click on links more if fear is involved.

If no person is literally bleeding, reporters will often pursue other types of harms, especially those created by institutions. And the easiest and most exciting institutional harms to investigate and report on will often be the failures and mistakes of government agencies.

This type of reporting gets the public outraged because citizens believe their taxpayer dollars are being used wrongfully or going to waste. These reports feel like a scandal and cause a lot of drama in and outside the institutions. This of course means more papers purchased and more links clicked, thus fueling the profits of the media outlets sharing the information.

The problem is that some media staff and editors will over-focus on the failures of these institutions and play down the successes. Some have termed this approach "*Gotcha* Journalism." "Gotcha" refers to the tendency of some reporters to search so hard for scandals and villains who are intentionally manipulating the system that they sometimes miss the truth: most employees are doing the best they can under very harsh conditions and sometimes make honest mistakes.

These whip lashings in the press end up creating a sense of fear, dread, and panic energy among leaders in the institution. One wrong step and they could become the next very painful public example. As a result, many leaders tend to move into a sense of "Command and Control"-style leadership, thinking that if they can control everything all the time, they will be able to limit the number of mistakes made and eliminate the possibility of negative media attention.

The great irony is that the more leaders are in a state of panic and fear around making a mistake, the MORE likely they are to make a mistake! That's because they are constantly in a state of fight or flight survival mode, so they don't have as much access to their higher-level brain functions like logic, problem-solving, and rational thinking. This becomes a self-reinforcing cycle.

Perhaps the most harmful aspect of the cycle is that this carousel of malfunction is highly contagious and rolls downhill. One leader of a large urban city office says "this type of behavior sets the tone for the whole agency." Leaders start taking on the *gotcha* mentality themselves as a protective layer to keep themselves safe. They look for mistakes and shame those middle managers who don't do everything perfectly or who don't meet their own personal standard of achievement. The middle managers then repeat how they have been treated to the front-line staff. In the worst-case scenarios, everyone is walking around traumatized, triggered, and MORE likely to make mistakes on a daily basis.

The Theater of Attack Politics

Most elected officials work diligently to win their campaigns, using every strategy at their disposal. They fully understand that obtaining positive media around their efforts is key to getting re-elected. Unfortunately, once a politician makes it into office (unless they are the President of the country), attention from the media doesn't come easily.

One elected official confided in me that it felt impossible to get reporters to pay attention to anything he did that created positive change for his constituency. He had pushed through dozens of bills and performed many activities that had profound positive impact. Yet the only measures the reporters were interested in were the issues where there was contention. If there was an angry community group or a backlash to one of his bills, the press was there in a jiffy with bells on. But work across partisan lines to generate a bill that the community believes is beneficial—media silence.

He recognized that this occurs because humans are drawn to drama and drama sells papers. He also admitted that in order to get media attention, some politicians would revert to creating their own flavor of drama. The easiest way to do that is to find a public servant to scapegoat and eviscerate in public.

Many elected officials learn quickly in their tenure that to keep their jobs (i.e., get re-elected), they must engage in *gotcha* politics. This belief manifests itself by calling out people from different parts of the system in harsh and dramatic ways to solicit media attention. Most of the time, this tactic is successful. These politicians obtain the media they are seeking and are seen as fearless leaders holding agency leaders' feet to the fire, to make sure citizens are receiving the services they deserve!

Holding agency leaders accountable when appropriate is necessary. When leaders are made aware of important issues that are causing great harm and are continuing to ignore the issue, then a strategic and well-orchestrated public campaign may be warranted to inspire leaders to change their tune quickly to address the issue.

The problem is that in some circles, this strategy is used as the first resort and not the last. Leaders don't get a heads up from a politician or opportunities to change course from the press when mistakes are made. Instead, when they are called out publicly for not addressing a particular situation, it is often the first time they are hearing about it. This not only creates confusion and trauma for the leader being chastised, but also initiates toxic culture within the institution, which actually leads to worse outcomes for the elected official's constituents. But the politician got their headlines!

A New Kind of Power

Negativity Bias

The media and media-hungry politicians play a large role in the creation of *gotcha* mentality. But it's not fair to disparage them for being at fault. Most of them are acting in alignment with one of our most annoying human traits—the negativity bias. It asserts that our typical reaction to any new piece of information is to focus on what isn't working instead of what is working. For example, if we get 99 pieces of feedback saying we did a great job presenting a workshop, and one piece of feedback saying we did a poor job, we tend to focus most of our attention on the one piece of negative feedback. If it's particularly bad, we might even dwell on it for several days rather than feeling good about how many people were thrilled with our presentation.

This also applies to how we view others. If someone in an institution is doing 99 things right and one thing wrong, we will often fixate on the one error rather than see the whole person and how much value they bring to the organization. The problem this creates is that when someone makes a mistake (as all humans do), leaders, the press, and the public tend to overemphasize the problem at the expense of seeing the big picture. We get so irritated at that one human for this one moment of imperfection that it discounts all the other significant work they've been accomplishing.

The other side of this phenomenon was articulated well by musician Don Henley in his hit song "Dirty Laundry," when he sings: "People love it when you lose, they love dirty laundry." This phenomenon is also sometimes referred to as "schadenfreude"—the tendency to take pleasure from other people's misery. It's not one of our most virtuous traits as human beings, but it does help explain why the media and the public are so obsessive in efforts to look for the failures of others. Perhaps it's just another form of the Blame Game. If we point out the shortcomings in others, we feel like we are keeping ourselves safe. And that feels good—even if it is a false sense of security.

Addiction to *Gotcha* Mentality

Over time, this *gotcha* approach to leadership becomes habit. Some leaders have even admitted to being addicted to this mindset. Paulina, a mid-level manager going from a toxic "Command and Control" government culture to one that is much healthier and more geared towards "Engage and Inspire" leadership says:

> *"I know it's better. I'm much less stressed out and I can do more thoughtful and better work here. I'm treated better and I'm healthier. But sometimes I crave the old place, and I don't know why... the energy was intoxicating."*

When Paulina went further to describe her experience, her story reminded me of a gambling addiction. The adrenaline rush of constant panic energy, combined with high-stakes decisions and not knowing when or on whom the axe would fall, is a powerful force. If someone is lucky, they come out of the day unscathed, feeling on top of the world and powerful. Their brains reward them with a large dose of dopamine. If unlucky, they'll feel the wrath of public humiliation or get fired and lose everything. It's an all or nothing game. Obviously, this is not a healthy way of living, but anyone who's ever known a gambleholic knows that they find it difficult to leave the game no matter whether they are winning or losing.

Let's solve the problem together...

Realizing how psychologically unsafe things can be in agency culture is depressing. There are many well-entrenched issues that make the condition feel irreversible. But do not fear. Luckily, this is a solvable problem! And of all the problems to address in this book, this one happens to probably be the easiest (and the least expensive) to solve. Here are a few ideas for how to do it:

1. Agree and Make a Plan to Create a Psychologically Safe Space

If you do not have a psychologically safe space but want to create one, an easy way to move forward is to bring leaders and team members together to discuss the issue and make new agreements around it. You can begin by describing what psychological safety is and discussing why it's so important in the workplace. If possible, it's ideal to offer opportunities for employees to share their difficult experiences without judgement (or fear of retribution). But don't stop there! Refocus the conversation on developing proactive plans for what to do in the future when mistakes are made. How will leaders react? How will team-members react? Don't be hesitant to get specific! Most people aren't taught how to respond well when things go south, so the more specific you get, the more likely the plans will succeed.

Don't expect it to flow smoothly at first. Our brains' neurons have been following down the path of blame and shame for many years. It takes quite a bit of practice and mutual support to get accustomed to responding with compassion and clarity when bad things occur. This is why the agreement part is so essential.

If someone inadvertently has an "old" style of reaction (and they likely will in the early days), others can simply remind them of the new agreement, which should help them reorient their brain in the moment. Possibly, they will need more practice before they can respond the way they would ideally prefer. Either way, having an agreement with a specific protocol and support for helping people move from knee-jerk reaction to thoughtful response is a game changer for government institutions. Mistakes become launch pads for learning and growing rather than fostering fear and scapegoating.

For example, Kenyatte Reid and Gillian Smith at the NYC Department of Education Office of Safety and Youth Development used a simple protocol called A.R.T. The entire 80-person staff came together to talk about building psychological safety and agreed to use the A.R.T. protocol to support the transition. When someone makes an error and a leader or colleague reacts with the "old" style of blame and shame mentality, other team members agreed to step up and engage in these three steps articulated by the acronym A.R.T.:

A - Acknowledge the pain of those who will suffer because of the error.

R - Remind those individuals that everyone makes mistakes.

T - Turn the conversation toward problem-solving.

That's it! This one agreement has helped move the organization into a higher level of psychological safety by raising consciousness on the topic and providing support for everyone to help make the transition.

2. Leaders Modeling Behavior

Regardless of how worthwhile the plan, there is one aspect that will make or break your team's ability to create a psychologically safe space. That is whether leaders are willing to model it! If leaders say that mistakes are expected and helpful opportunities for learning, but are themselves too nervous to share when THEY make an error, the psychologically safe environment will not work. The program does not function if the leaders aren't willing to walk the talk.

Of course, it is harder for many leaders in strong top-down environments to be open to admitting mistakes because they themselves are highly scrutinized by their leaders or the media. Accepting responsibility for admitting one made an error can feel like a difficult predicament. Leaders must be prepared to take the heat from the top, but at the same time be willing to create a cool, safe space for employees below them. This is probably the largest hurdle of being a truly Human-Centered Leader right now. One must be able to straddle both the "old" world and the "new" world at the same time.

However, nearly every Human-Centered Leader who has been interviewed for this book has suggested that being open about their mistakes with their team is a critical step to enabling the type of atmosphere where their team can feel free to take risks and thrive.

3. Well-Being and Mindfulness Initiatives

Lack of psychological safety at work can wreak havoc on our mental health and well-being. It also reinforces the inherent negativity bias in our brains. But these brain patterns are not irreversible. In fact, some government groups are helping employees identify and unlearn old, destructive thinking patterns and behaviors resulting from years of cultural conditioning in the workplace and replace them with more healthy, positive, and productive ones. This includes helping employees and leaders more effectively manage their emotions, recognize and work through trauma, and identify and navigate potential triggers that cause fight or flight thinking. In addition to creating healthier individuals within the workforce, this type of practice has the capacity to foster a healthier workplace culture and better outcomes for the institution.

One leader who has been successful moving such work forward is Dimple Dhabalia, former Senior Advisor for the Refugee, Asylum, and International Operations Directorate (currently the founder of Roots in the Clouds). In 2017, Dimple initiated a leadership and well-being initiative at the Directorate called RAIO Thrive. Based in mindfulness and positive psychology, the programming reflects a research-based, holistic approach to living well and flourishing by focusing on the physical, mental, emotional, and relational aspects of well-being as well as mindful leadership. Her mission was to keep the workforce resilient by equipping them with the knowledge, tools, and skills needed to promote positive change, practice brave leadership, and live and perform more intentionally.

RAIO Thrive offers a variety of programs, trainings, and resources to engage and empower members of the workforce to maintain their health and well-being while cultivating a culture of connection, compassion, and belonging within the Directorate. Thrive workshops focus on everything from making self-care actionable, to stopping our inner critic, to action-planning and goal-setting—all of which are critical to personal, professional, and leadership development.

Dimple started the initiative as a result of her own experiences. She found herself struggling to navigate issues like vicarious trauma and burnout from listening to stories of trauma and torture from asylum seekers and refugees day in and day out. When she first experienced symptoms of vicarious trauma while on assignment, she didn't feel like she could talk about it at work. Recognizing that others working at the cross-roads of government and humanitarian sectors were likely experiencing similar issues, she advocated for a program that would serve those serving the most vulnerable populations in the world.

Since Thrive is completely voluntary, Dimple was thoughtful about how to recruit others in the community. She recognized that there are a lot of misconceptions related to words like "mindfulness" and "positivity," including that they're "soft skills" that don't contribute to the mission. They are too often dismissed and devalued in comparison to hard skills and tangible metrics. For this reason, she intentionally designed a program that focused on evidence-based strategies and tracked various metrics to assess progress. This allowed Dimple and her team to provide concrete data that demonstrated program impact which helped develop credibility across the organization and get leadership and workforce buy-in. It also helped to normalize the need to acknowledge and support mental health and well-being in the workplace.

As a result, people in the office who might otherwise roll their eyes at talk of well-being began to acknowledge that the program is not about emotional fluff or toxic positivity. Rather, they understood it is about real, measurable growth that is helping employees develop new patterns of thinking, ultimately creating a better professional experience and wider pathways to leadership.

4. Proactive Partnerships with Media and "Beat the Drum"

While some government leaders have a deep-seated fear of media *gotcha* moments, others have figured out a way to get on top of the issue.

The U.S. Department of State Public Affairs Counselor, Alexander Daniels, developed a formula that has been extremely successful in addressing *gotcha* mentality. At the heart of his team's success is a primary principle of Human-Centered Leadership. Acknowledge the media as real human beings! Develop relationships with the reporters of the media sources that have you in their sights. Get to know them as people and understand what they believe, what they know, and where their gaps in understanding are. Take the time to fill in the blanks for them so they have an improved sense of the organization. This doesn't lead to a multitude of "feel good" pieces. But it hugely increases the odds that reporting will be fair, honest, and more nuanced so that a number of wins get in to balance out the challenges.

Alex also suggests the powerful strategy of repetition, or as he calls it, "beat the drum." Continue putting out press releases with positive stories several times a week. Don't be deterred if they don't get picked up immediately. Keep putting them out there. You can take different spins on the same hopeful story or announce a series of unrelated positive stories. Either way, the repetition of positivity will eventually register in the neural pathways of reporter brains. Once registered, reporters can more easily move beyond the negativity bias and will be more interested in sharing the entire truth with the public.

Whatever the strategy, having a proactive and intensive approach towards positive communications appears to be one key for unlocking psychological safety. At least a third of the Human-Centered Leaders interviewed for this book have explicitly hired communication teams to do bridge-building work with reporters and put out a constant barrage of positive press releases. One organization even held a high-end institute to educate reporters on the specific nature of an initiative, which led to much more effective reporting (and better outcomes for the initiative).

5. Media Resiliency Teams

One team in a government institution (which unfortunately did not get permission to be named in this chapter) decided to tackle this issue head on by creating a media resilience team. That means whenever bad press comes to pass, the team acts quickly to address the issue through three strategies:

1. come together in a judgement free and supportive space to identify the root causes of what went wrong in the system that led to the bad press and come up with a game plan to address it immediately;
2. develop and send communications telling "the whole story" to all affected employees and key stakeholders at all levels of the organization; and
3. focus on performing the work, supporting one another, and agreeing not to get pulled into the fallout of negative reporting which so often derails important efforts.

The "whole story" communications described in #2 above are always sincere, transparent, and positive in tone to keep morale up. But they doesn't shy away from the hard stuff. There is always an honest account of where mistakes are made, but no names are mentioned and no scapegoats identified. Instead, they discuss how the team is pivoting to address the mistakes made and support positive movement.

These communications also often include a quick overview of other things that are proceeding smoothly on the team or in the organization. It's like free PR! People read the memo or article because of the scandal, but they leave the article curious about all the great things happening. In short, it's allowing the institution to take control of the narrative. (Note: this only works if the institution is willing to own and address the mistake first.)

This approach allows those in the community an opportunity to feel positive about the overall organization, improves trust by being transparent about the more challenging issues, and models what it looks like to have a solutions-oriented culture that values and learns from its mistakes.

6. Educating Elected Officials

In an interview with Dan Garodnick, a 12-year member of the NYC City Council, we discussed the harsh effects of politicians screaming at agency leaders for various mistakes during public hearings purely to get media attention. I mentioned how those moments end up creating or exacerbating toxic culture by taking away psychological safety at the most senior levels, and how that toxicity cascades downhill to thwart initiatives. Through this discussion, Dan surprised me with these important words:

> *"I don't think elected officials always realize the harm that's done in the theater of attack politics. I think a lot of them wouldn't do it, or at least wouldn't do it as often, if they knew the damage it does to these institutions."*

Some of us might assume that politicians who engage in bouts of public shaming know very well how the humiliation affects various agency leaders and how that shame passes down into the culture—and just don't care. But perhaps that is off-base. And more importantly, perhaps this creates an opportunity for us to embrace a new strategy. If we can take the time to educate politicians so that they understand how these traditional public flailings end up hurting people, policy, institutions, and ultimately outcomes for their own constituents, perhaps that would significantly reduce or—if one is feeling optimistic— even reverse the trend.

Let's wrap it up...

In summation, government institutions with psychologically safe environments breed teams that are efficient, nimble, innovative, and wildly successful. Government institutions without it struggle with Blame Games, paranoia, corruption, information hoarding, lack of transparency, abysmal decision-making and, if history is at all an indicator, put themselves on the precipice of disaster at any given moment.

The lack of psychological safety in so many government institutions is the result of a series of root causes that have evolved over time. Some of these root causes include the negativity bias, *gotcha* journalism, the theater of attack politics, and our brain's reaction to the fear that is generated by all of these practices.

The good news is, this is probably one of the easiest and least expensive problems to mend in government culture. All it takes is bringing people together to CHOOSE to do things differently. We recommend specific protocols to help people make the transition, but all that's really needed here is a willingness to let go of the old way of doing things and an openness to trying something new.

For those who want to go the extra mile, initiating positive, human-centered relationships with media, developing media resiliency teams, and educating elected officials could go a long way in reducing (or even eradicating) some of the *gotcha* journalism which is at the heart of this matter.

One thing is for certain: if no one steps up to take on this role, the tyranny of psychological UNsafety will continue to fester alive and well across much of our government sector.

Reflective questions for team discussion

This section is designed for groups of people within an organization to discuss and explore options for initiating Human-Centered Leadership strategies.

Pre-Reflection Prompt for Team-Building

Why are so many people obsessed with kittens on the Internet?

Chapter Reflections

1. Have you ever been in a space with a lack of psychological safety? What did that experience feel like?
2. In what ways might personal experiences with a lack of psychological safety contribute to the way you lead and/or treat others?
3. Does our institution have more of a psychologically safe or unsafe space currently? How does this manifest? What are the outcomes of this type of environment?
4. Are there pockets within the organization that have more psychological safety than others? Why is this the case? What are leaders doing to create this space? Can it be replicated to other parts of the organization?
5. What would it take to begin discussing psychological safety across the organization? Are we at a point where we can get agreement among leaders to commit to creating a space of psychological safety?
6. What strategies might we consider that would help us address some of the root causes of a lack of psychological safety? What resources might we need?
7. What is one thing we can do right now to create more psychological safety on our team or in the organization?

For those who would like more information and resources on how to implement the Human-Centered strategies or ideas discussed in this chapter, go to centerfortransformingculture.com/resources.

Chapter Four

Paving a Human-Centered Path Towards Equity and Inclusion

Let's set the stage...

Last year, José's mouth dropped. José was Senior Director of an agency overseeing transportation in a major city in the Northeast. The Office of Equal Opportunity requested a report on the number of women in leadership positions,[17] which he assumed would be a non-issue. But, when he received the report from his staff, he realized a problem existed. Over 92% of the leaders in his institution were men.

José was a strong proponent of women in leadership, so he was flabbergasted at the numbers. But he was aware something had to be done to address the imbalance quickly or risk-taking heat from the mayor, who had made women's rights a key issue in his election platform. Subsequently, he did what he thought was right. He asked his middle managers to create a fast-track program designed to support women in the organization to help them better prepare for and access leadership positions. The program that subsequently got created included extra coaching, a dedicated community of support, and paid time off work to network with high-level leaders.

When the program started up there was an immediate backlash. Several men in middle management became angry. They felt this approach was unfair to them. Many of these men had worked their tail off to advance to their middle management positions. They had spent countless hours away from their families and worked tirelessly seeking to get into the good graces of the higher-ups in an effort to be promoted to a leadership position. They never received any time off or extra coaching support. They certainly hadn't received easy access to leaders. When they saw women getting what they considered special treatment, and possibly getting better access to the small number of jobs they were vying for, they pushed back.

The pushback came in different forms, but it made life harder for some women who were working for these particular men. Sometimes these women would be assigned more demeaning tasks in what seemed like passive-aggressive retaliation. Some would get scolded or talked down to in a humiliating way in front of the team. Some received negative evaluations even though their track records were stellar. While the women's fast-track program was meant to create more equity, the aftermath of the action seemed to be having some harshly inequitable outcomes for women while also fostering a toxic and disrespectful culture.

Todd, one of the leaders on the team implementing the fast-track program, said his heart was heavy with this development. He states:

> "Equality is easy, equity is hard... meaning, giving everyone access to the same things is great. But creating spaces to help give folks a leg-up that haven't had as much opportunity, so it's a more level playing field, that's a lot harder."

In terms of the way our brains work, Todd's comment is spot on. If everyone feels they have access to the same opportunity that generally feels fair. However, the moment people perceive others have more opportunity than they have access to, that's inevitably going to create a sense of unfairness.

In this case, many perceived the current state of leadership to be unfair because the organization was obviously (consciously or not) giving preference to those who happened to be men—hence, the 92% statistic. However, the men pushing back felt the women's fast-track program was unfair because they as individuals had worked incredibly hard on their own without any additional support. They felt strongly that everyone should have to reach the same standard without special treatment or access.

Unfairness, it turns out, is often subjective and can be sliced many different ways. Yet if the perception of unfairness is not addressed, it can stoke conflict, exacerbate inequity, and create major problems for workplace culture and outcomes.

This issue plays out in distinct ways across different contexts all the time: affirmative action policies, diversity recruitment efforts, school admission exams, etc. Tempers become heated on all sides of the topic. Each perspective runs under the assumption that they have the ultimate moral authority on what is truly fair. And once someone feels fairness is on their side, empathy for other people's perspective often gets tossed out the window.

Few stop to take a breath long enough to look at the root causes that undermine our ability to see fairness from different angles and develop empathy for perspectives beyond our own. Until we address these deeper-level issues, we will never be able to move the dial fully on issues of equity and inclusion.

This next section seeks to review some of the root causes in organizational culture that inhibit effective dialogue and meaningful action on the subject of equity and inclusion. The discussion will get thorny at times. Do not despair as we are only discussing them in detail so that in the subsequent section we can offer solutions that bring everyone on board and support a unified vision for equitable, inclusive, and positive change across all contexts.

Let's unpack the problem...

There are a large number of patterns that the neural pathways in our brains use to sort information when issues of equity surface. They are typically called biases. These biases are almost always on an unconscious level. Nobody knows it's happening while it's happening. But the harm these biases inflict can have catastrophic results for institutions and the humans within them.

The four brain biases below represent some of the biggest culprits for thwarting equity and culture in the workplace:

Similarity Bias (AKA "Us vs. Them" Mentality)

Back in the days of cavepeople, there was a lot of competition for survival around things like food and shelter. Tribes developed social bonds and trust based on "likeness"—those who were the most like them. That created a fear and distrust of those who showed "difference." That fear often prompted battle lines, creating an "us vs. them" mentality. Unfortunately, this trend has not died out during human evolution. At least not yet. When an organization points out differences among staff based on identity, it can create fear which triggers the amygdala function of our brain and launches us into survival mode or fight or flight thinking.[18] This survivalist mode leads to fragmentation of employees into opposing sides, squashes empathy, obliterates logical thinking, and fosters mindsets that demonize those perceived as the "other side."

Confirmation Bias

Once the battle lines are drawn, people start looking for negative intention and information to confirm that their side is the correct one and the other is in the wrong. They might begin looking for data in the news or in research reports that support their opinion, which bolsters their sense of righteous indignation. Of course, if someone only looks for data that supports their opinion, they are going to find it. (Most humans unconsciously ignore any data that could possibly challenge their current beliefs.)

But confirmation bias doesn't only apply to the written word or formal research. The search for information to support one's current beliefs and opinions becomes more personal than that—especially if office tension or conflict has already begun. We start looking for information that indicates those on the other side of the conflict are not just wrong... but malicious and evil.

For example, let's say during a meal at the Transportation office, one of the women in the fast-track program passes the ketchup with a bit of dribble down the side. One of the men on the other side of the conflict assumes she is trying to ruin his new white tie, which causes him to feel angry and more resentful of the program. The anger occurs in spite of the fact that a little dribble is quite typical on Ketchup bottles (unless you are a pro at hitting the 57 mark). Most likely, she had zero intention to ruin anyone's outfit. But because the brain is looking for data to confirm that those on the other side of the conflict are evil, it is perceived as an act of aggression.

Confirmation bias makes threats feel much bigger than they actually are. And the act of looking for and assuming negative intentions of people from the "other side" causes both sides to become triggered much quicker. This creates deeper division among employees, reduces access to empathy, and makes listening to one another almost impossible.

Group Think

This brain phenomenon describes our fear of saying anything outside of what our peer group believes to be the "norm." We fear that if we disagree with the opinions of those in our own community (or those perceived to be on "our side") that we will be cast out. That's a scary proposition considering much of our feelings of love, respect, and identity come from these communities. It's easier and psychologically safer to go along with what the group thinks is right. Unfortunately, this means that even if there were one or even a few men in the Transportation Department who believed it would be better to collaborate with the women than to act out against them, they are not likely to articulate those opinions for fear of losing favor in their community.

Zero-Sum Game

This brain effect uses math to describe some of the reasons for why we become emotional on issues of equity. It states that in any given situation, if one side wins an advantage, the other side loses one. So rather than seeing the Transportation Department's fast-track program as a chance to improve opportunities for women, the aggravated men perceived it as the taking away of opportunity for them. The truth is more nuanced. But because of the other three biases described above, the brain tends to revert to all or nothing sentiment when issues such as these surface.

Combined, these brain patterns make the path towards equity and inclusion difficult. The efforts that seek to create more equity without addressing these brain triggers can lead to major challenges in workplace culture. Collaboration becomes difficult, if not impossible. Conflict and negative emotions distract employees from performing well. People begin sabotaging each other's efforts. And any unified vision for success can go up in flames in the blink of an eye.

It may feel overwhelming thinking about all the issues that make equity and inclusion in the workplace hard to address. Luckily, this is a solvable problem! Many organizations have begun to figure out how to address these root causes in ways that create positive change without all the psychological trauma and drama that tends to go with them. We seek to explore these strategies with a few key examples below.

Let's solve this together...

The strategies below provide real-life examples of things leaders in government institutions are doing to create more equity and inclusion while at the same time developing trust, strong culture, and a unified vision of success. All of these strategies might not be appropriate for you or your workspace. That's okay! But if even only one works in your context, it could bolster your equity initiatives and foster that long-needed sense of unity and belonging among staff that we all crave.

1. Include Unusual Suspects in the Design of Equity Initiatives

Inviting Naysayers to the Table

According to many of our Human-Centered Leaders, if you create an equity-based initiative to provide resources that are meant to serve a particular group, it will be better received if leaders begin by inviting everyone to the table to participate in the design. This strategy builds on what some call the "Ikea effect"—people value something more and are more supportive of it if they have a part in the original construction. In effect, it means that when designing initiatives, ask people from all parts of the organization (including cynics) to weigh in and everyone will eventually see themselves as allies. This works because it obliterates "us vs. them" and "zero-sum" thinking that triggers defensiveness. People can't rally against the other side if everyone sees themselves on the same side.

This strategy includes inviting highly respected individuals who are staunchly opposed to your equity initiative to the advisory board overseeing the initiative (especially the ones who would be most likely to stir up trouble around it). This might seem counter-intuitive, but giving these naysayers a voice in the design has a number of advantages.

First, by including their opinions from the beginning, these individuals feel accepted, rather than rejected, by the community. That makes them less defensive and creates a space where they can openly discuss where they see challenges. Once they feel heard about the challenges, they are able to open up to comprehend the benefits of the work. As a result, they often become the strongest supporters of it. I've seen this happen over and over.

Even if some hardliners aren't willing to join the team, these individuals will feel less invested in organizing a team of people against it. They might not ever become true allies, but because their opinion was sought and valued, it takes the zeal out of their desire to push back on those leading the initiative. Your offer of an olive branch (if viewed as authentic) serves as inoculation against those who would otherwise come out to harm your work later.

Second, because these naysayers are on the design team, they can point out initiative obstacles, often better than others who are dewy-eyed with optimism or overly focused on one specific pathway towards outcomes. This perspective helps initiative leaders understand the language and actions that might cause other skeptics to react negatively in the future. Being aware of this information is critical in the design phase. It allows the design team to make modifications that obviate the now-foreseen obstacles, thus giving the team a much greater likelihood of full organizational success in the future, without getting mired in pushback.

Case in point is Erica Mohr, a former Commander who led a transformative Women's Leadership Initiative in the U.S. Coast Guard. As a Senior Officer in the service with considerable rank, Erica often found herself shielded from the more blatant sexism and harassment in the institution. She could have avoided thinking about the topic. But her defining moment came when she was seated next to a man on a plane who happened to be a roommate of a woman who was still junior-level in the Coast Guard. He asked her, "so do you also get sexually harassed on a daily basis?" She recalls the story, saying:

> *"In that moment, I recognized I had been promoted out of the problem. And that was the moment I was inspired to make a better Coast Guard than the one I was invited to join at 22."*

She had felt a fair share of sexual harassment in her early days, she recalls. And she said that's where she learned that coming out guns blazing could actually backfire and hurt her own career. So, as a leader, she decided to take a different approach.

She and her team used a radically inclusive approach to the design of the Initiative. She created an advisory board that included participation from leaders across the continuum of support for women's issues—from strong allies, to skeptics, to those with more traditional (and even some problematic) beliefs about gender. This broad base of perspectives and support enabled her initiative to get traction, even though it pushed back on some of the "alpha-male" beliefs and practices that were still very present in the organization.

She didn't just get their support at the beginning, though. She kept them in the loop at every turn. While she and her team did all the heavy lifting of creating the content for the Leadership Initiative, she would regularly go through a feedback process where she asked for input at every possible opportunity from all the key stakeholders. She would listen to that feedback, make the appropriate modifications, and made sure to communicate to everyone how their insights had strengthened the initiative.

The feedback and subsequent changes took time, but it was worth it because she recognized that this wasn't about operational efficiency—it was about prioritizing human-connection. She was showing each and every stakeholder that their thoughts and feelings mattered. Even if it meant including some elements that she didn't feel were important, or always agree with. She recognized that the relationship was just as important as the strategy. So she made sure to include their insights and support an abundance of communication, no matter how busy she got.

When the Women's Leadership Initiative held events, they always invited male Coasties (Coast Guard officers) to participate. Of course, many men chose not to attend the events. But the fact that they were invited was enough to dampen (if not eradicate) the "us vs. them" and zero-sum mentality. So it didn't become a thing. Those men who did attend said that they became more understanding and supportive of the work and felt grateful to be able to play a small part. They also expressed the value of experiencing the feeling of being a minority in a room, some for the first time.

The Initiative was launched with great success, with practically no backlash. Erica believes that there probably were some male officers who were not comfortable with the Initiative, but because of the inclusive approach and huge levels of support they had across the leadership continuum, those outliers never got traction. Instead, the Initiative blossomed into a national organization with thousands of volunteers around the nation that continues to this day. The effort was, in fact, so successful that other parts of the military (i.e., the Navy, Army, Air Force, etc.) replicated the model and began their own versions of women leadership initiatives.

Perhaps even more pertinent is the commentary by Laura Delgado, a younger female officer interviewed for this book. She suggests that because of the Women's Leadership Initiative, while there's still a long way to go on this issue, at least when sexual harassment in the military now rears its ugly head:

> *"Women now know, even on their boat—even on their first tour when they know nothing, they know they can fight it... and they can have power. So, they don't have to accept it anymore."*

In the end, because the Women's Leadership Initiative used an inclusionary and non-combative approach, they didn't get big headlines in the papers... but by golly did they make waves.

One-on-One Trust-Building Conversations

When talking about equity, some folks like to focus on systems of scale. That's the fancy way of saying making change large enough to affect a lot of people. Inclusion and equity are essential elements of thriving workplace culture for everyone in the institution, so seeking to create change at scale is a critical part of the picture. Yet getting leaders to support big changes usually requires a smaller one-on-one approach.

That's because people's hearts are much more open to change when there is meaningful interaction with someone they trust. That's true for politicians and leaders of government agencies, as well as pretty much all humans. If the trust isn't there, or if people feel blamed in any way during a discussion, they are going to stop listening. And if someone is feeling attacked based on how you present your case on equity, they are not likely to support you or your proposal. In fact, they are likely to double-down on their current beliefs and work more actively against your efforts.

That's why most of the Human-Centered Leaders interviewed for this book have chosen to utilize the one-on-one trust-building strategy as the method of choice for increasing equity in their institutions and communities. For example, let's look at the case of Gabrielle Hurtado (Gaby), who is the Medical Countermeasures Coordinator overseeing the COVID-19 Vaccination Program for the City of Long Beach's Health and Human Services Department.

Gaby quickly realized what many government leaders were seeing across the nation: many low-income communities of color were being hit hardest by the pandemic. The disproportionate numbers of hospitalizations and deaths in the community was heartbreaking. But instead of feeling frustrated and throwing her hands up in the air, Gaby decided to work closely with community partners and do something constructive. She and her partners initiated a full-fledged outreach campaign to improve access to services and win the trust of the community in ways that would improve health throughout the duration of the pandemic.

One of the plans required police officers to model and encourage people in these communities to better understand the safety and effectiveness of masks and vaccinations. Asking them to take on this role wasn't the usual way of doing business and required additional resources. The timing wasn't making things easier. The rollout of her team's effort happened about the same time that Black Lives Matter was gaining steam. Between the protests and media frenzy, tensions and distrust were particularly high between the police and the community.

Gaby could have been anxious that some police might be reticent to engage with the community, as the "us vs. them" mentality was escalating across both sides. Instead of giving into any fear, she went straight into her plan using the Human-Centered route. She decided to schedule meetings with police sergeants and lieutenants one-on-one. These were critical personnel to get on board because they had power to influence the front-line police officers on the ground. They represent the middle managers which research has shown are the key to successful change.[19]

She went out to lunch with them, spent time getting to know them personally, and built a relationship with each one. When enough trust was built, she presented data. The data showed why Black communities in the area had been disproportionately affected by COVID—showing stats on things like lack of access to health services, higher exposure to the virus based on their jobs, and distrust of the vaccine after historical mistreatment by the medical community.[20] She helped these police leaders see where the fear and distrust for medical institutions came from within these communities. Pointing that out created a sense of empathy among these police leaders.

It's important to note that the data that Gaby provided focused exclusively on the medical profession. The information was completely disconnected from any police data, which we know is an incendiary topic and could quickly trigger these leaders' fight or flight mode. If she had included even one data point that focused on police brutality in poor and Black communities, that could have very quickly made these individual lieutenants and sergeants feel attacked and get defensive, and that would have dismantled the effort to keep more people healthy in these communities. Her willingness to focus on potential points of being allies, rather than points of contention, is how she began to build trust that resulted in positive action.

It's also important to underscore that she was meeting with each police sergeant and lieutenant one-on-one. That individual, genuine connection between two people creates a space for trust-building. If she had met with these police leaders in a group format, there was a chance that "Group Think" would have taken over and spoiled the plans.

That's because in this polarized state of our nation, people often feel scared to speak out against their community by showing empathy for those on the perceived "other side." Gaby's strategic approach to invite these leaders into the conversation as individuals created the space for human connection that bolstered their confidence and allowed them to see themselves as allies. As a result, not all, but a majority, of the department sergeants and lieutenants she spoke with fully collaborated in initiatives designed to improve mask-wearing and vaccination rates in these low-income communities of color.

The project with the police was only one part of a larger initiative that included a number of community partners and a host of other creative ideas to build bridges and support health in Long Beach. And together, their efforts paid off. Long Beach was one of the first jurisdictions in California to reach the White House target 70% vaccination rate. And some folks are saying that the comprehensive approach used by Gaby and her partners may have begun the process of rebuilding trust between the government, police, and community. There's a long way to go before deep trust can be built—they are still in baby-steps mode, Gaby suggests. But it does beg the question if Gaby's path of giving the police a proactive role as ally in a larger effort to support equity and healing is one worth considering moving forward.

2. Use Human-Centered Leadership Strategies

The heart of Human-Centered Leadership means transforming culture to support every person in being their best selves so they can do their best work. At the same time, the approach addresses many elements of equity and inclusion. The program accomplishes this by focusing on empowering the least heard voices in the organization (which are often disproportionately people from underrepresented communities) and giving them pathways to leadership and empowerment that typically don't exist elsewhere. Here are a few examples.

Human-Centered Design/Design-Thinking is a strategy discussed in Chapter 2 that encourages the engagement and invitation of staff at all levels to help government programs innovate to improve efficiency and outcomes. These efforts enable staff to take leadership on change efforts even if they don't have traditional access to positions of influence. In other words, those with the least power in the organization and those who are the most marginalized have the opportunity to strut their stuff, offer their ideas, and show their leadership potential. As a result, many leaders begin to take notice of those who weren't showing up on the radar previously. This opens up the talent and leadership pipeline of an organization, allowing a more diverse and inclusive pool of candidates to have a real shot at leadership positions.

Employee Mentoring is a strategy we discuss in Chapter 1 that provides an opportunity for leaders to coach more junior employees and support them in their career trajectory. This is a classic way to help cultivate skills, networking opportunities, and confidence for those who have not had opportunities for mentorship or access to leaders in the past. Mentees coming from less advantaged backgrounds may have the potential to build social capital (which helps them with visibility, influence, and obtaining promotions later), while the institution benefits by developing a strong cadre of leaders for the future.

Co-Creation/Collective Decision-Making is also discussed in Chapter 1 and uses cutting edge protocols to engage staff and leadership in collective decision-making efforts about issues that affect them. This offers a sense of choice and voice for those who have historically not had either in the institution. That provides a meaningful contribution to creating a more equitable and inclusive atmosphere. It also provides a space for distributive leadership (shared power), which allows employees at all levels to manifest meaningful change that benefits their own work, the mission of the institution, and the communities being served.

Psychological Safety, as discussed in Chapter 3, means that managers create a safe space for employees to take risks, make mistakes, and bring their most authentic selves to the workplace. Instead of chastising employees for being imperfect and different from the norm, leaders who create psychologically safe environments celebrate difference! This leads to a high-trust environment where employees at all levels, and especially those from under-represented backgrounds, feel comfortable speaking their truth and taking risks without fear of retribution or negative impact to their career. This leads to a more diverse and equity-minded workplace, deeper connection with the community, and exponentially better outcomes for the institution.

You could use any one of these Human-Centered strategies to improve equity and inclusion, while at the same time improving culture and outcomes for your organization. However, if you are feeling bold, you can try all of them at the same time! One such government institution using this multifaceted strategy is the NYC Department of Education (DOE).

A few years ago, the NYC DOE decided to make equity a top priority. This was based on the newly-elected mayor's platform at the time and the chancellor's passion for the issue. There was also a practical understanding that to implement school policies which ensured students had equal opportunity in life, the agency itself had to shift its way of doing things to truly live the principles of equity and inclusion.

The DOE understood that fostering a sense of trust among employees was a key part of this quest. As one equity leader suggested:

"You cannot begin to build a culture and mindset of equity, without first building trust and empathy that allows people to understand other perspectives."

So Yvonne Soto and her team at the Division of Human Capital, Office of Organizational Development, Talent, and Culture (ODTC) went on a journey to build that trust. They engaged in a program of activities seeking to foster choice and voice, deep listening, and deep engagement among employees.

Like most things NYC, the ODTC didn't dance around the topic—they went hard! The team initiated cross-functional mentoring programs that included conversations about equity, held courses on psychological safety, facilitated implicit bias trainings, created guidelines for more inclusive hiring, set up Employee Resource Groups (see Empowered Employee Groups below), and hired professional development companies to train managers on using Human-Centered Design and Leadership. To learn more about these programs, check out the NYC DOE story in Chapter 1.

However, the NYC DOE is a GIANT organization, with more than 130,000 employees, and is the largest school district in the country by far. Their size alone makes any type of change a daunting task. Yet their comprehensive and unyielding approach to creating equity through Human-Centered Leadership appears to be working. Many employees are noticing a shift. And those with the traditionally least heard voices are speaking up about their experiences. Here are a few snippets from employees:

> *"Those who weren't heard at the bottom of the organization are now unleashed and able to do great work. They feel more involved, more included, more informed."*

> *"We are becoming co-leaders. I'm not in top management, but I was empowered to take a stand to do what's right."*

> *"ODTC has actually listened. They aren't just a group implementing programs to thousands of employees, they are genuine about developing staff and culture."*

The process to create change in such a large institution may be slow. But the many ways Yvonne and her team have been fostering Human-Centered Leadership seems to be providing a tangible roadmap towards more equity and inclusion.

3. Create the Ideal Conditions for Discussion on Equity and Inclusion

While the Human-Centered Leadership strategies discussed in the last section can catapult efforts to support equity and culture, there's also a more nuanced story around how to develop trust when talking about hot topics. Here are a couple more strategies to consider.

Deep Listening and Empathy

The conditions for productive conversations about equity require both empathy and trust. Without it, discussions can collapse and turn into long-term resentments and conflicts that take the work off-track. With empathy, deep listening can take place that enables people to be open to changing their hearts and minds so that more equity, fairness, and mutual-support can take hold.

Deep listening works because it keeps the amygdala (fight or flight trigger in the brain) calm. Instead of people getting triggered, it allows them the freedom to self-reflect and not take matters so personally. That helps them to be open to new perspectives and make small incremental progress that leads to positive overall change.

While the process is slower than many people have patience for, some high-level experts have been using it to showcase impressive results. For example, renowned activist and blues musician Daryl Davis has used deep listening as one of his primary tools in convincing over 200 members of the Ku Klux Klan to give up their robes and leave the Klan. If asked, he would say he didn't convince them. Rather, he gave them the space that allowed them to be open to new ideas and convince themselves. "I allow them to be heard and that's what works," he says. Doing the deep listening upfront, he suggests, creates the space for trust to develop. That trust eventually creates an opening of hearts and minds to consider new relationships, perspectives, and even data that Daryl brings to the table later. His method is interesting. We encourage you to check out the documentary about his work on Netflix.

The question on the table right now, however, is how can we build enough trust to be able to talk about equity and inclusion in government institutions?!

Many Human-Centered Leaders tend to do a fair amount of legwork before jumping into equity conversations. For example, Matt Torell from one of the finance teams in the NYC DOE did a lot of upfront work to help his team unlearn old patterns of thinking and develop the emotional intelligence needed to create a space for empathy before they started talking about things like race and gender.

He would ask his team to talk about empathy. How does each person define it? How is it different than sympathy? How can one have empathy for a person or a group without endorsing their perspectives? How do we listen deeply and honor people's feelings and their experiences, even if we don't understand them?

Even though team-members were coming from very different viewpoints on critical equity issues, these early conversations helped each team member immensely to open up to hearing other perspectives. Matt then brought some data from a neutral source to further the conversation. The goal was not to get everyone to a point of agreement, but to foster conversation that helped increase empathy for all opinions in ways that strengthened the culture of respect, equity, and belonging across the team.

Developing Resilience

Resilience means different things to different people. In this context, we're defining it as the ability to move through challenging feelings quickly, without getting triggered, so as not to internalize or inflict harm. This becomes an important tool when doing equity and inclusion work.

For example, when facilitating conversations about equity and inclusion, most facilitators will establish ground rules or community agreements ahead of time. Two of the most popular agreements used are: "this is a brave space" (where people are encouraged to speak their truth) and "this is a safe space" (where people are allowed to make mistakes without fear of being derided or attacked). While foundational to the discussions, there's a small space between these two agreements that can cause trouble.

Sometimes when people speak their truth, other people feel attacked—even if the first person did not intend what they said as an attack. This leads those folks feeling attacked to become triggered into fight or flight mode, which makes them respond in somewhat harsh, self-protective ways. That harsh reaction then triggers the first person even more and the next thing you know, people are screaming, everyone in the room is feeling triggered and the important work gets derailed.

However, when organizations take steps to help people build their staff's resilience, employees have more control over their emotions and behavior. Employees literally learn the skills to stop their fight or flight triggers before they start. This helps them to respond with compassion when feeling attacked, rather than getting defensive and argumentative.

Plus, it reduces or eliminates the effects of other people's harsh comments on their own sense of being, so they don't experience trauma that can create mental and physical health issues later on. That keeps everyone in a clearer headspace, which allows for more empathy, deep listening, and opening of hearts that leads to changed minds and more equitable policies.

A number of agencies have already begun hosting resilience workshops and offering resources, including the Center for Leadership at the U.S. Office of Personnel Management. They have multiple courses seeking to help employees develop their personal resilience by building skills in things like stress reduction, emotional intelligence, and development of more effective coping systems in the current environment.

Institutional efforts to support resilience are not always about equity, though. Many agencies are seeing resilience work as a critical strategy for supporting all types of change. The workshops gained in popularity after the COVID-19 pandemic hit. But when organizations are seeking to support large-scale change work in terms of equity and inclusion, staff resilience can be a real asset.

4. Employee Empowered Initiatives

Currently, many institutional leaders feel like they are in a bind. If they try to create change that supports equity and inclusion in the organization, they run the risk of being seen as heavy-handed and not getting it right, which can make things worse. On the other hand, if they allow communities most affected to lead all the change, they often become disconnected from the efforts, which makes it harder to support meaningful institutional change later on.

One way to resolve this issue is to give employees the power to make decisions that affect them by providing the structure, resources, and support needed to assist them in putting those decisions into action. Here's a few ways to accomplish that.

Employee Resource Groups and Affinity Groups (ERGs)

ERGs are spreading quickly in government institutions. They provide a platform that allows people who fit into a self-defined category to come together—with funding—to build community and help each other out while serving and supporting the goals of the institution.

ERGs are entirely self-identified, which means they can come in any possible configuration (i.e., employees of color, LGBTQ+, moms, office admins, 55+, Human-Centered Leaders, etc.). The groups are generally provided a structure for development, leadership sponsorship, and some funding to pursue whatever activities they want to achieve their own professional goals and empowerment.

These groups tend to focus on providing a space for community, skills training, and building social capital within the organization. This results in many members feeling more equipped and confident to apply for (and achieve) promotions which they may not have felt they had access to in the past.

One of the cornerstone activities in ERGs is the networking events. This is where ERG leaders invite the institution's most leaders (and sometimes external speakers) to do meet and greets with participants of the ERG. These are super effective because it gives senior-level leaders who want to be allies a clear, specific, and tangible way to support the ERG—just show up! The leaders who do show up then get to know and build relationships with people outside of their bubble whom they might not have known or had access to beforehand. This helps to address the "Networking Gap" (discussed in Chapter 1) which has historically made it much tougher for people with marginalized identities to access leadership positions.

Because ERGs tend to produce strong, mutually-supportive communities, there's a secondary benefit. When those from the ERG community get hired, they are likely to tap back into the community to help others get hired as well. They are empowering and lifting one another up, rather than having to rely on the altruism of leadership alone.

Together this creates a domino effect, ensuring people who were off the radar screen have the potential to move up quickly. For example, a co-leader of the ABLE ERG (Admins Building to Lead Effectively) which represents low-salary employees in a large urban agency, said that she had about a dozen employees call her and tell her they got promotions because of activities or networking from the ERG in the first few months. A dozen placements helping low-end salary employees rise up and get better jobs in the institution? That's an extraordinarily effective pipeline! And that's only the ones the leader had heard about. All it cost was the initial set-up of the ERG and a commitment of leadership to support their efforts.

DE&I Initiatives

Diversity Equity and Inclusion (DE&I) efforts have begun popping up everywhere. The number of staff dedicated to DE&I has more than doubled since 2015,[21] and DE&I committees are in so many government institutions and corporations now that it is almost uncool not to have one. The committees are usually voluntary but create a supported (and, ideally, funded) space for people who want to help the organization improve in the area of diversity, equity, and inclusion.

These spaces are powerful because they represent a sanctioned opportunity for employees to come together to talk about things that have before gone unspoken. It also provides a space for employees to closely examine and modify institutional policies that may be perpetuating inequity. For people within marginalized communities, this can provide a healing space—as past silence around issues of equity has been one of the perpetuating factors of "minority stress" and trauma among these communities in the workplace. But it also offers a platform to enable employees to take action in ways that help the institution become more equitable.

Many of these groups are in their nascent stages of development and still figuring out how to navigate a path forward to make equity more tangible. These endeavors can be difficult. But when there is a group of committed and passionate people coming together regularly to support positive change, it can generate a lot of ripple effects and help organizations move the dial on equity.

ERG and DE&I as Advisory Councils

A few organizational leaders have begun seeing ERGs and DE&I Committees not just as powerful instigators of bottom-up change, but as critical resources to guide top-down policy in areas affected by policy. For example, in many institutions, when George Floyd was murdered, Black and People of Color ERGs were key players in designing the institutional response—from what position to take, to what to say in the emails to staff, to how to create a space for listening and bringing healing to those experiencing trauma. These groups tend to have more empathy, knowledge, creative ideas, and emotional intelligence than traditional leadership teams who are further removed from the topics and often unsure how to proceed—so it's a win-win.

But it's not purely about responding to big events. It's also about identifying and recommending ways for the institution to transform at the systemic level. For example, many ERG or affiliation advisory groups have supported government agencies in making significant changes to hiring and promotion policies (see Chapter 5), transforming services to be more aligned with community needs, and engaging in efforts that create more connections with external change efforts (i.e., anti-bullying programs, wellness initiatives, etc.).

When people from DE&I groups or ERGs are tapped to serve as advisors, those with the least heard voices end up getting listened to and becoming equal players in the development of solutions to address systemic problems. As a result, the entire system benefits.

Of course, it's important to honor that if the individuals in any group are doing work to support the institution above and beyond their regular work-load, they should receive recognition of their efforts via promotional opportunities, bonuses, salary increases, or other methods. Otherwise, it could be perceived as an exploitative labor practice that reinforces inequity. But how and where to recognize that work can be up to each institution.

Amplification Strategies

This easy-win strategy came from Barack Obama's female staff. In traditional top-down government institutions, women (and folks from any marginalized community) struggle with getting access to and getting heard by those in power. A familiar refrain is that their ideas get taken by others with a more aggressive and dominant voice and they don't receive credit for their contributions. Often, those with strong voices don't know that they are usurping ideas from fellow colleagues (which is why it's often called unconscious bias). However, Obama's female aides decided to subvert this tendency with a simple, yet stunningly effective strategy they referred to as amplification.[22]

The female aides in Obama's offices came together and agreed that whenever one of them had a good idea in a meeting, the others would repeat the idea and give them credit for it. For example, "as Monique suggested earlier on..." or "building on Jasmine's idea, which was to...". The strategy worked! The simple act of reminding leaders where the ideas were coming from was enough to help the neural pathways of those in charge give credit where credit was due. They reported that the strategy led Barack and other leaders to start calling on women more often in meetings, and led to a lot more ideas being credited to the women who offered the idea in the first place.

5. Proactive Communication Campaigns

There is a very effective, but woefully underutilized, strategy for building trust and developing equity in most government agencies: communications! When government institutions proactively put strong positive messages out into the community, people tend to respond well. The messages don't have to be controversial or complicated. Simple showings of support for communities who have been underrepresented can be sufficient to make it known that the government is on the side of ensuring all community members deserve respect and fairness. When paired with intentional policies to support equity and inclusion, these showings of support can go a long way in developing trust between the government institution and the community, while at the same time sparking powerful conversations about equity across the region.

For example, in addition to going to bat for the community in the courts, the NYC Commission on Human Rights engages in regular communications campaigns. Their campaigns seek to reduce discrimination and improve their position as ally with communities across the city. They have already engaged in multiple campaigns focused on supporting the community in the wake of anti-Muslim and anti-Sikh violence. These campaigns included the creation of compelling graphics with positive messages and posting them across the city wherever they were able—in subway cars, on billboards, in social media, on buses... the works. They also paired the campaigns with efforts to get to know and learn how best to support the Muslim community using city policy and law—the agency's sweet spot. Here's a few of their campaign graphics:

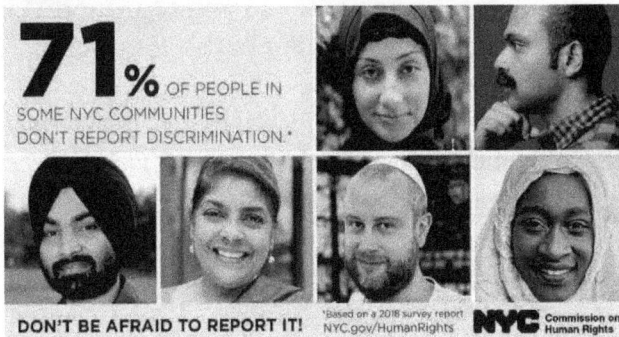

These types of messages are critical because even though a government agency has the intention of being supportive of various communities, their only way to traditionally show that support is via policy efforts. Unfortunately, the public rarely gets to see the amount of work that goes into policy development. Policies take a long time to push through (if they go through). Because communities don't see the effort, they often don't feel cared for by these institutions. These simple but powerful graphics plastered around the city are a great way to show that the government cares and is a strong ally of those communities who don't get much of a voice.

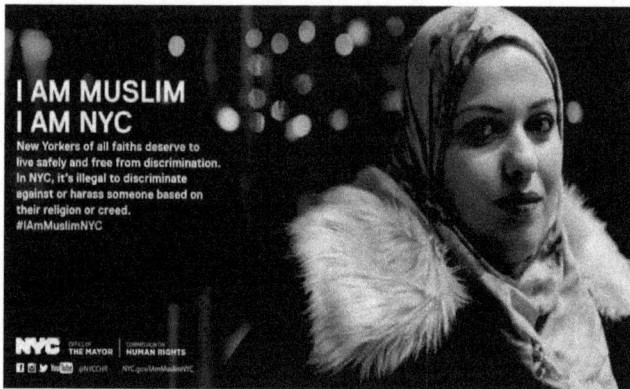

The Commissioner of the NYC Commission on Human Rights believes that these campaigns, in addition to their aggressive law enforcement, aggressive anti-bias efforts, and presence in the community, have been pivotal to turning around long-standing resentment and distrust of government in the community. The proof is in the pudding.

Many organizations and Muslim leaders had previously been active in publicly shaming and even suing the city because of perceived neglect and prior harms felt by the community. Yet because of her team's extremely hard work and a strong communications campaign, the Commission is now getting awards from those same Muslim leaders and community for their powerful support. The Commissioner gets emotional when she describes it:

"It's one of the proudest moments for me. That these entities—the government's biggest critics, who are used to suing the city—finally see that there's goodness here. That they have allies here, and that there's hope here."

One additional huge benefit of comprehensive communications campaigns is the knock-on effect. A general rule in advertising suggests that it takes seven impressions to influence the brain. That's because our neural pathways are more open to receiving messages when there is significant repetition of the new information. By spreading equity-based messages across the city, the institutions are actually helping citizens of the city become more likely to have positive thoughts and feelings about equity and inclusion. The communications campaign is literally making the city more equitable, just by existing.

Other organizations have sought this route. For example, Keith Richards (no, not THE Keith Richards from the Rolling Stones) is a great guy currently working as a leader with Discourse, an agency in Canada working on DE&I. About a decade ago, he worked with the Durham Police Service to improve relationships with the LGBTQ+ community. They had the idea to engage in a creative communications campaign by painting the outside of patrol cars with pro-LGBTQ+ images.

This was a proactive effort to build more trust with a community where some felt marginalized and mistreated in the past. The gesture was well received at the time. People would take selfies with the cars, generate memes (with a positive tone), and celebrate when one of the cars decked out in rainbows was in the neighborhood. While no one in the community thought it was a panacea that would heal all of the distrust that accrued over time, most saw the proactive and very visible effort as a positive first step. It also signaled to police officers with anti-LGBTQ+ biases that their way of thinking was not in alignment with the institution. That in itself was viewed as institutional progress.

Paving a Human-Centered Path Towards Equity and Inclusion

Important Caveat

Keith's partners at Discourse, Vishal Rampaderat and Chris Fernandes, discussed one of their critical lessons learned in their work with the Durham Police. They mention that communications campaigns work best when done in concert with other meaningful change. If there are no meaningful actions beyond the communications campaign, this approach could backfire.

For example, building off of the success of the LGBTQ+ initiative from a decade ago, Discourse leaders worked with the Durham Regional Police Service to paint various patrol cars with images of LGBTQ+ Pride, Aborigines Pride, and Black History Pride in 2017. The hope was to show good will and take some baby steps towards trust-building with the community. The gesture was received well by many when it was first unveiled. But backlash against the Black History Car emerged in 2021 during the first Black History month post George Floyd's Murder.

The cars were being called out by some in the community for being "performative." They were being seen as an isolated initiative, without connection to any visible policy efforts to address the bigger systemic issue that was creating trauma in the community: the disproportionate killing of Black people. Some argued it "felt like a slap in the face" which depleted trust with the community and created some negative press.

There are still a number of people who are supportive of the cars and believe it's at least a good starting point. For others it is still a bone of contention.

The moral of the story: communications can be a great tool for trust-building—if it goes beyond the paint job.

Let's wrap it up...

Creating equity and inclusion is one of the most difficult things one can attempt in a government agency, especially in today's context. Tempers run high and willingness to change runs low. It's a recipe for disaster that can easily take the work of equity off the rails and kill workplace culture as collateral damage. Even so, it is imperative that we figure this issue out, lest we be subjected to deeper polarization, less equity, and (even more) violent conflict in the coming years.

The good news is, Human-Centered Leaders have figured out considerable pieces of the puzzle for how to talk about and create equity in ways that foster good feelings and a unified vision for change. When leaders understand where the triggers are in each space and create steps to artfully walk around them, they can create the conditions to foster trust, deep listening, and empathy. This means the conversations get more productive, the equity work gets more traction and people feel rejuvenated from the experience, rather than battered down by it.

Different leaders do that artful walk using different methods. But some of the ones pulled out for your consideration in this chapter include: bringing unusual suspects to the design table on equity initiatives; using Human-Centered Leadership strategies; creating the ideal conditions for productive conversations; and engaging in proactive communications campaigns.

Many government institutions are deciding to choose a Human-Centered path forward towards equity and inclusion. The question is, is your institution one of them?

Reflective questions for team discussion

This section is designed for groups of people within an organization to discuss and explore options for initiating Human-Centered Leadership strategies.

Pre-Reflection Prompt for Team-Building

Please describe a fabulous lunch date. Who are you with, where are you, what are you eating?

Chapter Reflections

1. What is a time you felt you were treated unfairly? What happened and how did it make you feel?
2. How, in your opinion, do those feelings connect to what others experience in terms of equity and inclusion?
3. What strategies from what we read about might be able to help us think about or take action on making things feel more fair and equitable here in our workplace?
4. What obstacles might get in the way of those strategies?
5. How might we overcome those obstacles?

For those who would like more information and resources on how to implement the Human-Centered strategies or ideas discussed in this chapter, go to <u>centerfortransformingculture.com/resources</u>.

Chapter Five

Hiring Leaders with Emotional Intelligence (Using an Equity Lens)

Let's set the stage...

Janella intends to hire a Director of Programs for an innovative system of food distribution for shelters in the Midwest. She interviews five candidates and Neil really stands out. He attended Harvard, is quite articulate, passed the Civil Service Exam, and is considered an expert in matters related to food distribution based on his prior roles managing five-star restaurants in NYC. He has a brilliant vision for how to roll out the new distribution system and is confident he can pull it off. Moreover, he's charismatic and funny. Janella considers this one a "no-brainer" and hires him immediately.

Four months after he is hired, Janella learns a major vendor is pulling out of the project which could significantly stall the initiative. She knows someone at the vendor's office who could be helpful in resolving the issue. She calls Neil to see if her contact can help address the problem. He becomes weirdly defensive and angrily blames someone on the IT team. She's confused about how a miscommunication with IT could lead to this result, but is too busy to focus on it, so she moves on. Otherwise, during their regular meetings, he's reporting good numbers, projecting confidence, and things seem to be moving smoothly.

A few months later, she learns that another vendor is pulling out and four members of Neil's team are leaving the organization. She calls HR to see if they have any information. She discovers that Neil has been wreaking havoc in the department by yelling at employees, making threatening accusations, fudging numbers in his reports, and blaming vendors for mistakes that are apparently his own doing. In the seven months he's been there, he's created a toxic culture, lost two critical vendors, and some of the institution's most promising employees have quit because of him. He's no longer in his probationary period, so it will be exceedingly difficult to fire him.

This particular example was contrived to represent a critical problem in many government institutions. We hire managers based on a limited set of information. They look great on paper, speak well in interviews, and have all the requisite certifications and experience, then shazam! After they become settled, we learn they are extremely difficult to work with. Perhaps they are getting their deliverables out the door and producing outcomes expected for their office. However, it comes at the costly price of creating a toxic environment for those under them where employees feel stifled, traumatized, and are likely to leave the job (either physically or in their hearts). This is the opposite of creating a workplace that inspires a sense of belonging.

The interesting thing is, there are countless smart, passionate candidates ready to take on leadership roles who know how to get amazing outcomes AND support a thriving culture. The leaders who have this ability have what we call Emotional Intelligence. The term has been getting more traction in recent years. Emotional Intelligence is the ability to understand, navigate, and manage emotions (of oneself and others) to support the best outcomes for the most people.

Yet some of our government institutions continue to stick to the traditional methods of recruitment and selection. They haven't learned how, or haven't yet transformed their hiring practices to weed out the candidates who don't have Emotional Intelligence. Moreover, there are a slew of unconscious biases going on in our brains, making our chances of hiring spectacular leaders with Emotional Intelligence more difficult.

This chapter seeks to underscore some of the key challenges entrenched in our current process of recruitment and selection and offers some promising solutions to address them. The goal is that this knowledge will support a shift towards a more thoughtful and effective hiring selection process, which means better leaders and better government.

A New Kind of Power

Some Research for Your Consideration

Emotional Intelligence (EI) accounts for nearly 90 percent of what sets high performers apart from peers with similar technical skills and knowledge. It is twice as important as IQ and technical skills in terms of performance at all leadership levels. Further, 71% of hiring managers now say they value EI over IQ.[23]

The research isn't discounting technical skills or IQ. They are also valuable and critical to any leader's success. But as Daniel Goleman, author of one of *Harvard Business Review*'s most enduring articles on leadership, puts it:

> *"The most effective leaders are alike in one crucial way: They all have a high degree of what has come to be known as emotional intelligence. It's not that IQ and technical skills are irrelevant. They do matter, but mainly as 'threshold capabilities'; that is, they are the entry-level requirements for executive positions. But my research, along with other recent studies, clearly shows that emotional intelligence is the sine qua non of leadership. Without it, a person can have the best training in the world, an incisive, analytical mind, and an endless supply of smart ideas, but he still won't make a great leader."* [24]

Google, one of our planet's most successful technology-based organizations, did a review of their highest-achieving leaders with a result that reinforced Goleman's thinking. Ninety percent of the most common attributes among their top leaders all fell into the category of emotional intelligence—or what some refer to as "soft skills." You can check out the ten most powerful leadership traits they found here below: [25]

1. **Good coaches:** support their team members by providing encouragement, building on their strengths, and helping them grow in their challenge areas.

2. **Empowering team-members, not micromanaging:** ensures that everyone feels like a potential leader inspired to take their work to new heights, without someone breathing down their neck.

3. **Creating an inclusive team environment, showing concern for success and well-being:** fosters a space where everyone feels cared for and has a sense of belonging, and where there is intentional effort to reduce bias.

4. **Being productive and results-oriented:** helps employees understand what is expected of them, and ensures they know how to achieve it in the timeline provided.

5. **Being a good communicator, listening and sharing information:** communicates in ways that build understanding, supports transparency, and creates enthusiasm across the team.

6. **Supporting career development and discussing performance:** invests time and energy in helping each team member grow within and beyond their role.

7. **Having a clear vision/strategy for the team:** ensures everyone is on the same page and moving in the same direction towards a shared vision of success.

8. **Having key technical skills to help advise the team:** understands the components of each team member's job so employees can help when they need it.

9. **Collaborating across the organization:** stays connected to the bigger picture and collaborates with other teams to maximize results.

10. **Being a strong decision maker:** is able to look at all perspectives and data and then make the hard decisions.

The common thread woven throughout nearly all the Google study findings is that when leaders know how to listen to, develop trust with, and empower employees, they will succeed at much higher levels.

Plenty of other leaders advocate around this topic. The CEO of Campbell's soup, Doug Conant, says when he's looking for leaders, he looks at those who can build trust on their teams. He puts it this way: "Contrary to popular belief, cultivating a high-trust culture is not a 'soft' skill—it's a hard necessity. Put another way, it's the foundational element of high-performing organizations."[26]

Fortune Magazine tells us that "trust between managers and employees is the primary defining characteristic of the very best workplaces." They also suggest that these companies earn more money, with three times the annualized returns on the S&P 500 than other companies.[27]

Richard Branson, CEO of Virgin, says one of his three top leadership principles is about being an effective listener. He says:

> *"Listening enables us to learn from each other, from the marketplace, and from the mistake that must be made in order to get anywhere..."*[28]

It's not just about managers and leaders, though. Nitzan Pelman is the Founder and CEO of Climb Hire, a new recruitment and training firm which assists adults from diverse communities in getting out of poverty circumstances by going from low-salary jobs (about $24k) to moderate/high-paying jobs (about $66K). Climb Hire has been wildly successful, placing about 80% of their recruits in great jobs with major corporate giants like Nike, Salesforce, IBM, and Amazon. Nitzan says:

> *"What made us so successful is that we started investing in helping our recruits develop soft skills and emotional intelligence. I used to think it was all about technical skills, but I've learned that's outdated thinking. Employers value people who know how to build relationships, who know how to collaborate. Anyone can learn technical skills—and we teach those too! But we've seen that the most forward-thinking organizations want inspiring employees on their team— and that takes emotional intelligence."*

Hiring Leaders with Emotional Intelligence (Using an Equity Lens)

Let's unpack the problem...

Despite the many impressive advocates and a large body of evidence that shows emotional intelligence is a powerful predictor of effective leaders, current protocols in a large number of government agencies still focus on those who can get the job done—rather than who will be an inspiring leader AND get the job done.

There are a number of surface-level issues contributing to the problem. The pool of applicants is usually too small and the time too short to try and find those who have the technical skills and ability to foster effective team environments. Moreover, it's unclear how to ask questions in ways that will help identify those who have high levels of emotional intelligence. Therefore, many continue utilizing the processes they have been using. Which means some leaders with extremely low emotional intelligence may get selected for leadership positions. As a result, culture and outcomes falter.

In this section, we describe some of the most powerful root causes that inhibit emotional intelligence in our hiring decisions. In the subsequent section, we discuss how to resolve them.

Confidence Gets Confused With Competence

We're attracted to people with confidence, both romantically and professionally. This is alluring because when someone has it, they give the impression that they actually have their act together. In this fast-changing and sometimes uncertain world, we feel safe and secure believing that someone at the helm knows what they are doing. We are anxious to put our faith in them so we can rid ourselves of fear of uncertainty and know that life will be perfect.

Here's the rub: confidence does not equal competence! Research indicates that those who have developed an extremely high level of confidence are often the least equipped to lead. This is especially true for those whose confidence is based on their expertise. In fact, people who are considered "experts" in any given field tend to have less accurate prediction skills than the average Joe, even when they don't have any experience in the same field. And the stronger the area of expertise, the LESS likely the expert is to make accurate predictions![29]

As *Forbes Magazine* contributor Greg Satelle aptly puts it:

> *"One of the things that makes experts so convincing is that they exude confidence. They can talk calmly and knowledgeably about a subject, make reference to relevant facts and build a compelling logic for their case. A good expert is always impressive, but still usually wrong."*

There are many high-achieving specialists in various fields who have a rich and powerful knowledge-set to bring to the table. It's important to appreciate and build on the critical information they offer to inform our policies. But it's also essential to have a critical eye towards those who are self-proclaimed experts and/or try to sell us on the idea that they know everything about a topic.

These types of "expert" leaders are well-meaning. But they are often inaccurate because they tend to rest on their laurels. They are so positive they figured out the correct answer in the past that they believe they will also be correct in the future. And because many people offer praise and articulate their faith in the expert's opinions, experts have little reason to question their own efforts. Ergo, they often stop testing their own assumptions, neglect new and updated information, dismiss alternate theories, and make decisions based on insufficient data that ultimately steers the work in the wrong direction.

Yet in many circles, expert bias wiggles into search committee activities through something called the "Executive Presence" indicator. This is basically the catch-all phrase for "does the person exude a kind of confidence that makes people want to follow?" It's a helpful quality to look for. A healthy dose of genuine confidence and ability to immediately influence others is a wonderful leadership trait.

Unfortunately, there is a slippery slope between healthy confidence and overconfidence, and very few of us are keen enough to know where the line is at any given moment. Further, when an interview panel does not have a protocol for weeding out overconfidence or expert bias, they are more likely to choose the candidates who are overconfident (because of that annoying sense of fear of uncertainty we talked about earlier).

There's another aspect that makes it more problematic to identify overconfident people in interviews. For most of us, when we are the ones being interviewed, the thought of saying "I don't know" is unheard of. We are fearful it will come off as a weakness. We are supposed to know everything in an interview, that's why we are being hired, right? Instead of speaking our truth, we are taught to pretend that we know the answer. The mantra "fake it 'til you make it" is used in many circles to help those who are lacking in knowledge to find confidence. This greatly muddies the water both in terms of finding the people who actually know what they are doing, and weeding out the people who are so overconfident that it creates a problem for the organization. The issue penetrates our hiring practices so deeply that it creates additional negative knock-on effects.

Reducing the Applicant Pool

One of the prime problems associated with perpetuating the overconfidence bias is that it greatly diminishes the number of talented applicants applying for leadership positions. This manifests through an equity lens as well as personality.

From an equity perspective, women—for example—are much less likely to apply for leadership positions because they don't feel confident enough that they have all the necessary information.[30] Many believe their knowledge base is insufficient for becoming a leader, so they don't bother trying. Whereas men, in general, tend to be more confident that they will be able to figure out what to do even if they don't have all the information.

In addition, many with soft-spoken personalities believe that going for positions in higher echelons of management requires a disposition that is too different from their own. One study showed that those who don't apply for leadership positions avoid it because they characterize leadership opportunities as "self-centered, showy, and arrogant."[31]

Others have described the leadership styles of those in political circles as necessarily cruel.[32] These gentle-oriented individuals tend to shudder at the thought of being perceived as cruel or self-centered, so they stay in their current roles rather than try for more influential positions.

The irony is that soft-spoken individuals are most likely to be the ones that have a Human-Centered Leadership approach and therefore to be more effective leaders. They are the folks who can put their egos aside and focus on building their team in ways that ensure great work from everyone. They are the ones most likely to encapsulate the very leadership attributes extolled by *Forbes*, Google, Virgin Airlines, and the top companies in the Fortune 500.

It's unfortunate. The overconfidence factor in hiring decisions makes it improbable that those who have the Emotional Intelligence and skills to build a high performing team culture will choose to become leaders—and less likely that those with Emotional Intelligence will get chosen for those positions!

Narcissism

Another issue with over-relying on confidence or "Executive Presence" is that people with extreme narcissistic tendencies slip in without anyone noticing. Narcissists generally tend to be drawn towards positions with power since they thrive on influence. This increases the numbers of people with narcissistic traits in the applicant pool for leadership positions. They are also the most likely to be selected because they lean toward being exceptionally confident, charming, and have a strong sense of vision for success that is inspiring to be around (at first).

This isn't knocking those with narcissistic tendencies. Many of our world's greatest accomplishments have been achieved by known narcissists, from Napoléon Bonaparte to Tiger Woods to Mark Zuckerberg. A strong dose of narcissism can indeed be an asset when trying to make big changes in the world. Most people going after big lofty goals will have at least some narcissistic tendencies. You need to have an incredibly strong vision and unyielding belief in yourself to turn your vision into reality. The decision to hire someone with narcissistic tendencies should, therefore, not be discounted.

The danger comes in when people with extreme narcissism (or more specifically, those with Narcissistic Personality Disorder) get hired for senior-level positions. Folks who have developed this mental health issue can be super exciting and compelling in the early stages, but probably will do irreparable damage to the people around them and to the organization in the long run.

People with Narcissistic Personality Disorder (NPD) tend to gain power and influence because of their extremely charming personalities and bold (usually positive) visions for change. The problem comes in after they attain power and influence because they become very fearful of losing power and quickly become distrustful of those around them. This distrust turns into a coping mechanism called DARVO[33] which obliterates empathy, catapults conflict, and leads down a rocky and very dramatic road for institutions. DARVO stands for: Deny, Attack, Reverse Victim and Offender.

DARVO plays out when someone with the disorder feels threatened. Unfortunately, people with NPD feel threatened quite easily. Any hint of critical feedback, questions about their work, negative comparisons with colleagues or suggestions that there is a better way of getting something done different from what they are doing are all cause for feeling threatened. Once that threat kicks in, so does the amygdala part of their brain that goes into fight/survival mode.

Once in fight mode, they will typically respond with DARVO by Denying any mistakes, Attacking the individual who suggested they might have made a mistake, and Reversing the roles of Victim and Offender so that they seem like the victim of the mistake and the other becomes the unsympathetic perpetrator. Their movement through this process typically includes extreme verbal abuse, controlling behavior, lies, and master's-level manipulation.

There's also a typical practice of blowing things up by making (often false) accusations of others in the office which leads to dramatic outbursts and ruffled feathers. This technique puts them on the offensive, rather than the defensive, which helps distract from their own problematic behavior. This forces those working under the person with NPD to try to put all the pieces back together after the fallout of each outburst that tears things apart.

Unfortunately, DARVO has proven to be an extremely effective strategy that enables people with NPD to skirt out of perceived threatening situations. This pattern of behavior does irreparable mental health damage to all the people around them, creating anxiety, depression, and penetrating self-doubt that undermines good work. It also causes many people to leave the team, or bail on any project involving that individual. The overwhelming consensus from research is that the only way to effectively deal with a narcissist is to run away from them as fast as possible.[34]

For your institution, it means bad news because decisions are being made in survival mode (when the brain's access to logic and empathy is significantly reduced). A fair portion of decisions are instead being made out of jealousy, spite, revenge, and all of the other dramatic tendencies you think are only reserved for shows like House of Cards. Ultimately, having someone with NPD in your leadership will mean a one-way ticket to "toxic city" and misguided policy. In addition, it's likely that team members, vendors, and collaborating offices may quit or shift direction so they don't have to deal with that individual. This, of course, has the potential to reduce organizational capacity, stunt collaboration and make it extremely complicated to move projects forward.

The worst part of this equation is that most leaders do not even know who has NPD on their teams. This is because people with NPD are master manipulators. They can present data in ways that show they are being wildly successful, even when projects are crumbling around them.

The damage people with this mental health issue can do to the humans on their team and the liability they create for the institution is incalculable. Yet most leadership hiring protocols don't attempt to touch this issue with a ten-foot pole. As a result, some of these leaders sneak into powerful positions. And boy oh boy, if you try to get rid of someone with NPD who has power, put on a helmet and whatever protective gear you possess. You are going to need it.

Hiring Leaders with Emotional Intelligence (Using an Equity Lens)

The Peter Principle

The Peter Principle is a stinging endorsement of the idea that just because you are good at one job, doesn't mean you'll be good at the job you were promoted for. It suggests that "people rise to their level of incompetence."

While the tone of this principle is not entirely consistent with the tone of Human-Centered Leadership, the content is relatively aligned. In Human-Centered Leadership we understand that just because you are good at your job doesn't at all mean you understand how to manage a team of people in the same job. They are two entirely different skill sets.

For example, Wayne Gretzky was considered one of the best hockey players of all time. But that didn't mean he'd make a good coach. In fact, he made a terrible coach. He's been chastised in sports media for never getting his team to the playoffs and leaving the team in bankruptcy. His own team didn't even want to be associated with him when he left.

Just because you are good at your job, doesn't mean you'll be a good manager of other people in that job. And yet some government institutions continue to promote people for management positions based on their performance in another job, but who have not proven their aptitude for management.

However, unlike the Peter Principle (which insinuates people are hopeless at a certain point), Human-Centered Leaders believe that management skills can and SHOULD be learned. Wouldn't workplace offices be much more effective if all leaders ensured their middle managers had the opportunity to learn these skills, especially if they are not inherently present when hired? Who knows, maybe Wayne Gretzky would've had a real shot as head coach if he had just taken some Human-Centered Leadership courses before taking over the reins.

Implicit Bias

We think that when we hire people, it's based on our own well-researched facts, objective opinions, and sometimes our intuition.

Unfortunately, research is telling us that this belief is often false. We are learning more and more that subtle biases have penetrated our minds over time and unknowingly influence our decisions about hiring.

Perhaps the most prominent is the affinity bias. We tend to hire those who think, act, and look like us. This is a natural human tendency—we want to work with people who we would also want to hang out with. And we prefer hanging out with people who share our experiences and interests (because they think, act, and look like us). While understandable as a human disposition, this creates a large problem in hiring because it means that viable candidates may get rejected based on personal and subjective opinions that have nothing to do with their ability to do what is required to efficiently perform the job.

Implicit bias also creeps in based on our consumption of media. Media works based on the theory of repetition. A generally accepted rule in advertising is that it takes seven impressions to make an imprint in our brain. If someone sees your ad seven times, they are more likely to buy whatever you are selling, whether a box of Hot Pockets or a political candidate. This is why companies and politicians spend so much money on advertising—the more you see their message, the more likely you are to believe their message (regardless of whether or not it is true).

Over the course of our lives, our brains have been subjected not to just seven or eight impressions, but thousands of impressions that reinforce what media projects as "good," "beautiful," and "capable." As an example, while this practice has been changing a bit lately, leading male characters in the movies and TV still tend to be aggressive, opinionated, and emotionally stunted. Leading female characters continue to be demure, kind, and physically attractive.[35]

The impressions don't pertain only to entertainment. Our brains unwittingly transfer the images in the media into our daily life and routines, including when we are searching for people to hire. As a result, certain types of people are much more likely to get hired or promoted based on what the media deems valuable. For example, people who are perceived as attractive are much more likely to get hired those who are not.[36] Men who are tall are much more likely than short men to get promoted into high paying jobs.[37] Americans over 40 are half as likely to get hired than their younger counterparts.[38] People with White sounding names are twice as likely to get called back for interviews as those with Black sounding names.[39] Men are 1.5 times more likely to get hired than women.[40]

The list of biases goes on and on to the point where it becomes ridiculous. Incredibly, there is even a bias towards people who know how to slide the occasional rhyme into their conversational repartee!! It's called the Rhyme-as-Reason effect, meaning you are more likely to believe someone is telling the truth if they rhyme when they say it. I use this technique in Chapter 2 when I talk about "Spray and Pray" initiatives.

The point is, we have all been subjected to the images in the media that shape our thinking so we are all biased whether we like it or not. Recognizing that is half the battle. The other half is taking tangible steps to reduce implicit bias. If we don't agree to fight the battle, we are all likely to keep playing out these brain patterns at the detriment of a slew of amazingly talented humans who didn't happen to be born with the attributes currently valued in mainstream media.

Yes, this all seems quite overwhelming and sad. Luckily, this is a solvable problem! Keep reading and the next section will explain some quick and easy wins to make your hiring practices much easier, fairer, and far more effective.

Let's solve this together...

There are a number of government institutions that are moving the dial on hiring. They are finding ways to hire Human-Centered Leaders with emotional intelligence, high IQ, and strong technical skills. Some of them are doing so with a strong equity lens to ensure that new hires are diverse and representative of the communities being served. Here are some of the organizations and the work they are doing. As you read, you might consider which strategies might work in your own setting.

1. Build Your Team's Awareness of Bias, Then Co-Create Selection Process

Selection teams who interview candidates often include leaders and HR executives during the first few rounds. Sometimes the candidates get to meet the other team members, but that usually happens after a decision has been made or almost decided. However, when leaders bring in their team members to co-design and co-facilitate the entire selection process, it makes it much easier to find the right match while also building trust and effective collaboration skills across the team.

Leaders who want to ensure that their selection process is less biased can take the extra step to educate themselves first and then take the information to the team. To accomplish this, leaders bring in articles or research on the various biases that can pop up and facilitate dialogue with the team on how to avoid bias traps during the selection process. Then teams co-create protocols or strategies to put those ideas into action.

These co-designed protocols create a common understanding of what biases may get in the way and provide a strategy for how to avoid that happening. Further, because the team created the strategies together, there is a sense of community accountability to the process. Everyone is holding one another accountable for ensuring the anti-bias strategies are top of mind throughout the process. This makes the team's candidate choices a lot more fair, equitable, and inclusive than most institutions (which sometimes have only nominal head nods to diversity and inclusion).

For example, Matt Torell from one of the finance teams at the NYC DOE brought in articles about equity and talked to his team frankly about all of the potential biases that could come into play. He then worked with his team to co-design protocols for interviewing that reduced bias as much as possible. All of his team members were excited about the opportunity to attempt something new and figured out several ways to support the effort.

They scrubbed the names off the top of resumes to eliminate or mitigate bias, they created "tasks" so the focus of the interviews would be on how well candidates performed (not what they look like or where they went to school), and they collectively came up with questions and rubrics that helped elucidate if the candidate had a high level of emotional intelligence.

Additionally, the team participated in all of the interviews together, discussed the merits of each candidate, and had a process to come to a consensus at each round. Everyone had equal say and everyone on the team happened to be looking for the same qualities: someone they could trust, who would do the work well and with gusto. When the team ultimately settled on their hire, they felt like celebrating. They were proud of their collective decision and extremely eager to begin work with their new teammate.

In the end, I was lucky enough to meet their choice. All I remember thinking was that the match was so perfect that I wanted to kvell like my Jewish grandmother at a wedding, "I'm so happy you found each other, Boobala!"

2. Hire From the Community Being Served

It's a trade-off whether to hire from the inside vs. the outside. An outside hire can give the organization a shot in the arm because they represent a fresh pair of eyes, with a different set of skills or experiences and a new dose of energy. An inside hire means you are creating a cadre of leaders, building trust within the organization and creating wider pathways toward equity.

Carmelyn Malalis, the Chair and Commissioner for the Human Rights Commission in NYC, believes both pathways are possible. While it is important to offer the staff opportunities to grow in their careers by promoting from within, Carmelyn also looks to hire personnel from the community that their organization serves—not from a pool of external candidates with no relationship to the organization.

The Human Rights Commission has inspired countless organizations across the nation in their ability to amass power by partnering with the community (as described in Chapter 2). One of the additional benefits of this approach is that the staff is familiar with the movers and shakers in the areas they are trying to affect. They know the people from the community who are most respected, their track record of success, their leadership style, their skills, and their drive.

When the Commissioner's team needs someone to fill a position, they go to that community first. This makes the staff not only incredibly diverse (they speak over 30 languages in the office) but also extraordinarily passionate about the work. There's more at stake for these employees. They know every effort they make is an opportunity to help their own communities thrive. Hence, they work even harder to discover creative ways to get over systemic obstacles that inhibit meaningful change. They are creative, scrappy and go the full nine yards, every day.

The other benefit is that this government institution is truly representative of the communities it seeks to serve. That's not lip service. Everything the institution does will include the perspective of people from the communities. That makes all of their work better received, more effective, and builds boatloads of trust along the way.

Some folks may not be ready to take this leap. It's a big shift to ask leaders to start prioritizing community credibility over Ivy League diplomas. But it's hard to deny the Commission has benefited from this approach. The institution has gone from being called "toothless" and "moribund"[41] to becoming one of the most formidable and effective government institutions talked about today. They have won awards from historically underserved groups in the City, received media coverage at a level unprecedented for any Human Rights Commissions (with over 107 billion media impressions and over 6 million engagements), and are perhaps the only entity in the country to have figured out how to hold media accountable. (They successfully slapped a major news network with a one million dollar fine for their role in creating an unsafe environment for women.) They are killing it!

If there's anything this organization has demonstrated, it's that hiring people from the community is not just a nice thing to do, it's a pathway to meaningful community partnerships that helps build the credibility, effectiveness, and power of government institutions.

Hiring Leaders with Emotional Intelligence (Using an Equity Lens)

3. Encourage Those With Human-Centered Leadership Skills to Apply

As many government institutions are seeking to transform culture, most are looking to empower new and emerging leaders from within their organization that already have Human-Centered Leadership skills. However, not everyone with Human-Centered skills is looking for leadership positions. This means that leaders serious about shifting towards a new, Human-Centered model of leadership must spend extra time first to find and encourage potential candidates to apply.

Yvonne Soto and her team at the NYC DOE Office of Development, Talent, and Culture take steps to reach out to those who are the most likely to have Human-Centered leadership skills as soon as they know management positions will be opening. They do this through outreach out to the leads of their empowered employee communities letting them know when opportunities are coming up. Some of the empowered employee groups include: employee resource groups, affinity groups, DE&I committees, employee mentoring programs, advocacy groups, and more. Most of these groups are very active and excited to help people from their community improve access to potential promotions. Even just the heads up from Central office is enough to get great people into the pipeline (who may have been invisible to leaders previously).

The team also sends out notices to all employees who have taken any of their Human-Centered Leadership Courses. The organization offers dozens of courses each year where managers learn critical culture-building skills such as: how to give empowering feedback; supporting collective decision-making; creating psychologically safe environments; and more. They are even currently considering giving those who have taken Human-Centered Leadership courses an online badge to tag their effort, so they are more easily identifiable during hiring opportunities.

They do not merely focus on sharing knowledge of position openings, though. They also actively communicate with the leaders of various communities and course alumni to help identify the most promising emerging leaders and ensure they have all the qualifications necessary to attain the next-level jobs. This includes letting these potential candidates know when civil service exams are coming up, what skills they need to develop to meet job requirements, and giving them a bit of moral support and cheerleading to let them know their style of leadership is highly valued.

4. Use Interview Protocols That Emphasize Human-Centered Leadership Skills

Job interviewers used to go with their gut instinct when considering who would be a good fit. Unfortunately, research has been showing that these perceived reactions are more often a function of unconscious bias than gut instinct. As a result, opportunities to promote equity and Human-Centered Leaders have not been prioritized.

More recently, government offices have been creating systemized rubrics for interviewing to buffer against potential bias. These protocols provide a consistent set of questions and criteria that are asked of every candidate, in the same way, so as not to make it easier or harder for any particular individual based on unconscious bias. Typically, selection committee members rank each candidate based on the criteria, which is then tallied and considered the basis for whether or not the candidate continues on to the next round.

It's a great way to ensure clear and measurable assessments of each candidate. Unfortunately, most protocols continue to miss the opportunity for digging into the most critical indicator of success according to the research—Human-Centered Leadership skills (AKA "soft skills" AKA "emotional intelligence"). Sure, it's important to ensure candidates have the technical skills and experience for the job. But the odds of your manager or team member being able to achieve great success skyrockets if they naturally know how to build culture as they are doing their job. It's also helpful to ask Human-Centered leadership assessment questions to weed out any potential candidates with latent Narcissistic Personality Disorder.

The Marin County Public Works Roads Division has begun using a rubric that puts Human-Centered Leadership traits front and center. They've been using it to support their leadership team in finding hires who can bring in new technical skills while also supporting the positive culture they are attempting to create.

Here's a short excerpt of a sample hiring rubric similar to the Marin County version, focusing in on the emotional intelligence piece. To access the whole rubric, go to the resources link at the end of the chapter.

SAMPLE Hiring for Human-Centered Leaders Rubric (Excerpt)

Interviewer Introduction to Leadership Scenario Questions

We are going to give you some scenarios to help better understand your leadership style. These scenarios suggest that you got and are currently in the job, and then posits issues in team dynamics that might cause bumps in the road. We're curious about how you might address them. There are no right or wrong answers, but we ask that you try to fill in the blanks where necessary and imagine the scenarios the best you can so you can answer as honestly as possible.

HCL Skills	Possible questions to ask interviewees	Things to look for
Psychological Safety	Let's say you are planning an event in three months that the public and leaders are coming to. The person on your team taking the lead on the project finds a location, recruits a panel of well-established speakers, and finds a new vendor to provide free snacks. You are happy with the progress, but the day before the event, you learn that only 3 people have signed up to attend	<u>Human-Centered Approach</u> -Do they work quickly with the team to find ways to solve the issue as best as possible? Do they express empathy for the person who made the mistake? Do they engage in efforts to use this as a learning opportunity, helping the team ensure the problem does not happen again in the future?

	because your lead didn't let people know about the event. This is a critical error. The leaders are expecting a good showing, and you are going to be very embarrassed when only a handful of people attend. How do you approach the situation? What do you say/do to the lead? The team? The Leaders?	Traditional Compliance Approach -Do they focus on blaming the person who made the mistake? Do they emphasize punishment and accountability for the error they made?
Effective Feedback	Let's say there's an important deadline to get a report done by the end of the week summarizing the results of your team's work. Almost all staff members have gotten you the summary of their efforts with highlights of their successes in the timeline you asked, but one team member has been dragging their feet. Their slow pace is making it hard for you to finalize the report and is threatening the future of the team. If you don't get the report in on time, the whole team's budget may get substantially cut for the upcoming year. How would you handle that?	Human-Centered Approach: -Do they have the emotional intelligence to first engage with the employee to learn why the they are dragging their feet? Do they explain why it's so important? Do they offer support to help them get back on track? Traditional Compliance Approach: -Do they immediately resort to compliance mentality and punitive consequences to get them back in line?

Collective Decision-Making	Let's say one of your team members who addresses a lot of the clerical work is taking off for maternity/paternity leave. You aren't able to hire a temp, so the team needs to step up and take over much of their workload for the next few months. That means adding more work to your already heavily taxed staff. The staff aren't going to be happy with the situation. But you need to make sure that the team doesn't lose functionality. How do you decide which employees have to take on the extra work?	Human-Centered Approach -Do they invite the team-members to have a say in how the work gets distributed? Do they give them a platform to discuss their frustrations? Do they try to find a fair way of doing it and explain the process they used? Traditional Compliance Approach -Do they simply come up with the plan on their own and tell the team they have no choice? Do they only tell them to "suck it up" and just do it? Do they suggest they can get another job if they don't like it?

Let's wrap it up...

In conclusion, government institutions can create a much faster pathway towards equity and Human-Centered Leadership if they become more strategic and intentional about how they hire and who they hire. This requires a shift away from traditional old protocols which rely too heavily on technical skills and certificates, and miss what the research says will lead to the most successful candidates—people with emotional intelligence. It also requires a move away from our human tendency to assume that confidence equals competence, and let go of our unconscious biases that seep into our decision-making processes.

A New Kind of Power

The good news is this massive shift is actually not that difficult nor that expensive to pull off. A number of government agencies are taking recruitment and selection to the next level and showing us how it's done.

Some are working with their own teams as partners to develop protocols that reduce bias and find candidates the whole team can trust. Some are finding candidates from the communities they serve, which develops more power for both the institution AND the community. Some are recruiting from internal groups that focus on lifting employee voice, while providing guidance for employees who innately have (or proactively seek out) Human-Centered Leadership skills. And some are using protocols specifically designed to assess employee emotional intelligence, in addition to technical skills and experience.

While none of these strategies alone are sufficient to turn around culture over the short term in any given institution, they each support a much more important trend: a paradigm shift in the type of leaders we value and empower to lead our government.

Reflective questions for team discussion

This section is designed for groups of people within an organization to discuss and explore options for initiating Human-Centered Leadership strategies.

Pre-Reflection Prompt for Team-Building

If you weren't doing the job you are doing now, what would be your alternate profession?

Chapter Reflections

1. What does our hiring and promotion process currently look like? Is it consistent or all over the map?
2. What hiring and promotion practices do we use that we believe are good for our institution?
3. What practices do we use that are getting in the way of hiring Human-Centered Leaders?
4. What practices do we use that are getting in the way of hiring with an equity lens?
5. What would a Human-Centered Leader look like in our institution? Who do we know that might be described as a Human-Centered Leader?
6. How do we get others in the institution to become supporters of a new selection process?
7. What can we do right now, either large or small, to support movement towards practices that will help us find, recruit and select super effective leaders who will attain outstanding results for the institution, while supporting a more equitable and human-centered environment?

For those who would like more information and resources on how to implement the Human-Centered strategies or ideas discussed in this chapter, go to <u>centerfortransformingculture.com/resources</u>.

Conclusion

This book was written at an auspicious time. The world continues to reel from a global pandemic, workplace dynamics are shifting, civil unrest is prompting new conversations, fires are raging out of control, Wall Street is proving vulnerable, and most of us are just hoping that the world will change for the better as a result of it all.

The challenging part is, we don't know how to change. We don't know what positive change looks like. That means we aren't sure where our world is headed or what exactly comes next.

We do know that change is scary—even on a good day. But when the very foundation of our world feels at the precipice of collapse, it is absolutely terrifying. Some people will push back on that change as hard as they can, holding fast to old ideas and old standards that once provided a sense of safety and security. Those who are more comfortable with ambiguity will head into the tsunami of change with open arms, navigating the tricky waters with a sense of intrigue and hopefulness.

Most of us will land somewhere between these two spaces. Some days, we will feel brave and have the strength to move forward, other days, we will feel nervous and need to retreat to protect ourselves. But there is one thing that is for sure at this point in time. If we fail to seize this opportunity, if we do not build on this powerful chance to make a meaningful shift that makes life as we know it better, we will have missed the greatest opportunity for positive change that our generation has ever known.

For deep change to take place, however, we need to better understand the journey. First, we need to establish a destination point that we know everyone can get to. That begs the question: is it possible to establish a common vision for positive change, in spite of a nation (and perhaps a globe) that currently feels so polarized? If we can figure that out, the next step is to figure out the vehicle—how we're getting there. What are the skills and knowledge we need, as individuals and institutions, to help us shift our ways and realize that common vision for change? And last, but not least, we need some fuel to keep the vehicle in motion to ensure we can get from here to there, without petering out.

Conclusion

The fuel comes from the passionate, strategic, and determined Human-Centered Leaders who drive us to where we want to go, and make sure everyone gets there together.

Perhaps you are one of the Human-Centered Leaders who can help us get to the destination point. If this book has resonated with you, maybe this is the time for you to help pave this road to positive change—at least in the workplace. If you aren't sure, just consider these two questions asked by ancient scholars and U.S. presidents:[42]

If not you, who? If not now, when?

The authors of this book seek to empower those with a yearning to find new ways of doing things in government institutions. We offer new ideas, new strategies and new ways of thinking about power, that can radically transform not what government institutions do, *but how they do it*. That one small shift can offer wildly better outcomes for the institution, the employees, and the communities being served by them.

If you are nervous about stepping forward, do not fear. This type of change, for the most part, does not require a large budget. Nor is it even that complicated to pull off. You will find friends and supporters along the way that want to join your cause, and that will bolster your efforts and your resolve.

The toughest part will no doubt be the mind shift. For this new kind of power to take hold, the majority of people working in government eventually need to adopt a new way of thinking; a philosophy that prioritizes the development of a strong learning culture and values each and every human being's potential to accomplish greatness. They need to be open to trying new leadership strategies that inspire trust at all levels and ignites employee passion. Lastly, they need to understand that they can significantly improve government outcomes simply by lifting up and listening to the voices of those who work within government.

This new way of thinking is called Human-Centered Leadership. It has the power to change our understanding of what is possible. As the title of this book suggests, this new kind of power can help government institutions become more innovative, more equitable and create a deeper sense of belonging that attracts and retains top talent. But as the stories described over and over in this book suggest, it does a lot more than that.

As we read about in Chapter 1, government agencies adopting this mindset are creating better infrastructure for employee choice and voice, inviting people at all levels of the system to become co-designers in the work of change. As a result, these intuitions are experiencing large returns on investment through increased productivity, decreased sick days, more nimbleness, better collaboration, more empathy (across historically divided communities), and a much more engaged and inspired workforce.

In Chapter 2, we explored how forward-thinking agencies using Human-Centered Design are making it much easier to innovate and improve systems efficiency. The leaders in these institutions have figured out quick and easy ways to ensure information is flowing up, down and across the organization so that problems can be anticipated and addressed in record time. These leaders showed us how to create environments where employees take initiative to solve tough issues and innovate in their own spaces regularly. We saw that when their methods were applied to the surrounding communities, it inspired a deeper sense of trust and belonging among the very people the institutions seek to serve.

Chapter 3 is perhaps the most vital in the book, as it focuses on the cornerstone of Human-Centered Leadership: creating psychologically safe environments. This chapter lays out exactly why psychological safety has been missing in government agencies, and then offers some quick, easy, and FREE strategies for addressing it in meaningful ways. Using these strategies, a number of Human-Centered Leaders have created spaces where everyone feels brave to speak their truth and learn from mistakes. Along the way, the agencies doing this work are also helping employees show up as their most authentic selves, sparking innovation, offering leaders some well-earned breathing room, and receiving positive press.

Conclusion

Chapter 4 is perhaps the most relevant in today's climate. Focusing on how to create an atmosphere that supports equity and inclusion, this chapter offers a powerful set of stories and strategies that show how government institutions are winning hearts and minds—without ruffling feathers. These institutions are empowering the least heard voices, and in doing so, creating wider pathways to leadership. They are turning around naysayers, and winning awards from the community for their efforts. They are responding in more nuanced and responsible ways on highly charged issues such as race, gender, and sexual harassment, and creating ways to reduce (and heal from) bias. They are also creating a space of empathy across the organization, so that deeper listening and understanding can take place across communities of difference.

Finally, Chapter 5 offers a slightly different pathway to making Human-Centered Leadership the new normal. The groups in this chapter show how to locate, hire and promote leaders who are emotionally intelligent—in addition to being very smart and having the right technical skills. Some of these leaders are doing this work while using a strong equity lens. The institutions engaging in these efforts are seeing a lot of perks from their efforts, including: an increase in the number of effective leaders across the institution; more inclusive pathways to leadership; an uptick in new employees who match the culture of the team; a more diverse and more committed staff; and much less likelihood that people with Narcissistic Personality Disorder end up in influential positions.

Together, these chapters provide a roadmap for anyone working in government institutions who is bold enough to seek positive change. Each chapter represents a potential starting point that can be used to initiate conversations and momentum to get the ball in play on Human-Centered Leadership.

However, these five chapters don't represent the totality of what Human-Centered Leadership has to offer institutions. One of the key principles of Human-Centered Leadership is not overwhelming people with too much information at once. This book seeks to be a starting point, and not a destination for those searching to foster positive change in government culture. There are many more pieces of the puzzle that are mentioned in the book, but not explored in an in-depth way.

We encourage you to pursue resources elsewhere (or wait for the author(s) to write Volume II of this book) to learn about other concepts that also fall under the umbrella of Human-Centered Leadership. Some of these might include:

1. *Performance Feedback*: Giving and receiving feedback in ways that empower employees AND improve performance.
2. *Initiative Pace*: Learning how to slow down the pace of initiative rollouts to improve success rates and keep employees in top form.
3. *Information sharing*: Moving from becoming presenters of information ("Sage on a Stage") to facilitators of knowledge in ways that honor all voices in the room ("Guide on the Side").
4. *Bridge-Building*: Helping to resolve tensions and build trust among teams or communities in conflict.
5. *Community-Building & Wellness:* Creating opportunities for joy, connection and wellness across the institution.

The world of Human-Centered Leadership is indeed in its nascent stages. But the number of leaders using these strategies is growing every day. If you feel called to help your organization move to the cutting edge of this new type of leadership, we invite you to take a look at the free tools and strategies offered in this next section and consider which option might be something you can begin using immediately.

Strategies to Bring Human-Centered Leadership to YOUR Institution

The work of shifting an institution towards Human-Centered Leadership is a relatively new idea. It's happening in pockets around the country and gaining steam around the world. However, getting all the leaders in your organization to buy into the idea, and prioritize the implementation of these new ways of leading, is no easy feat. Such an effort will require time, intention, patience, and a concerted effort of a small, committed group people to tip the scale in favor of a new way of doing things.

This may feel like a mammoth task. You might be questioning whether you even have the capacity to take this on. There is one thing that can be said with confidence: you are NOT alone. There are people everywhere, from all walks of life and all types of jobs, who know in their heart there is a better way of supporting institutional success. A way that is more aligned with their values. A way that is closer to that vision of a better post-pandemic world. Many of these people have been hoping, waiting for an entry point to create that shift.

If you are one of them, consider this book your entry point. And consider the tools and strategies below to see which, if any, might help you initiate this important work. Perhaps one will resonate and that will be your path forward. Or one will spark another idea forward that can catapult your efforts. Regardless of who you are—whether a front-line worker, middle manager, or leader—the next steps you take may determine whether your institution moves towards a new, more humane and effective kind of power, or whether it stays stuck in the past.

(Strategies for Managers or Leaders of Teams.)

1. Use Book as Team-Building Activity

This book was designed to support meaningful conversations that help managers and their teams work together to create a high-performing team culture. To support this end, we've developed a set of Reflective Team Questions and a link to potential resources at the end of each chapter. The questions were crafted to facilitate high-level critical thinking, honest dialogue, and collective ideas to improve the team's culture. We also include a fun ice-breaker question at the beginning to help build community. The potential resources offer additional readings, strategies, and services that can help teams go from discussion to action.

To turn the book into a team-building activity, simply ask your team members to read the book. Then set up five meetings to discuss the reflective questions after each respective chapter (you can throw on extra meetings if you want to discuss the introduction and conclusion). We recommend 45 minutes for the discussion.

Team-Building Activity Bonus Item

For those high-achievers who want to try out an effective Human-Centered Leadership strategy from the get-go, use a shared-leadership facilitation protocol for the Team-Building Activity. It's a bit more structured, so it can feel prescriptive to some. But those who use it say the intentional process often leads to more engaging and productive conversations. To use it, simply ask team members to volunteer to take on different leadership roles for each chapter discussion. Here are some leadership roles you might consider:

Facilitator

This team member is generally well-organized and/or good at bringing groups together. Ahead of time, this team member identifies which questions to ask from the book and determines the timeframe given to answer each question. They also are the ones to ask the identified questions and stoke conversation. And most importantly, they are the one making sure that all voices are being heard and honored during discussion.

Timekeeper

The ideal person for this job is someone who feels empowered by rules and believes in keeping people on-task. The team member with this role keeps things on track by occasionally reminding the team how much time remains to answer each question, based on the amount of time allocated by the facilitator. They need to have a firm voice, though— 'cause when people get passionate, it's hard to reel them in!

Pro-tip: Timekeepers may ask permission of the facilitator and group to extend certain timelines, if it feels like conversations need to go longer.

Conclusion

Culture-keeper

This team member should have a positive disposition. They offer praise in any format (i.e., high-five, "way to go," touchdown dance, etc.) to keep the vibes high when someone comes up with a great idea or when the team comes to full agreement on something. They also find ways to honor people's emotions during poignant or sensitive moments (i.e., "That must have been hard to say. Thank you for sharing," or "Thank you for bringing your truth into the room.").

Notes-keeper

This person should be a fast writer or a fast synthesizer of information. If a team chooses to take any actions based on the discussion, the Notes-keeper writes down the agreements about who is going to do what, and by when. Subsequently, they share those notes with all participants so the team is accountable to each other to ensure the commitments are kept.

Reporter

This team-member is typically an extrovert. They are responsible for sharing the key takeaways from the discussion with other people in the institution. This can include leaders or colleagues in other offices to help spread word and create buzz around the great things happening on your team (just make sure to keep confidentiality, where appropriate).

Your team can redesign the activity above in any way it feels appropriate. Perhaps you are able to create different kinds of leadership roles. Or instead of everyone reading the whole book, divide up the chapters among team members and have them present on what each person learned. It's up to you! The activity is meant to be a guide, not a mandate. We do recommend that you ask your team members what they think first! It's much more Human-Centered to invite them to help craft the activity with you rather than dictating all the elements—and will earn you a lot more enthusiasm for the activity.

(Strategies for Leaders or HR Directors.)

2. Conduct a Culture Survey and have an Action Plan Ready!

To get all leaders to buy-in to the idea of Human-Centered Leadership, they need to understand that the current culture is not working as well as it could be. Most of the time, these leaders have no idea there is even an issue because they've been promoted out of the problem.

One of the best ways to help make the case is through data. You might consider developing or working with an external group to design and conduct a survey that assesses culture across the organization.

Heads up that you'll need to do a fair bit of work to help employees feel safe enough to take the survey and to be honest in their responses. A lot of employees have had bad experiences where speaking their truth has gotten them in trouble (see Chapter 3 on psychological safety).

We recommend making the survey anonymous, if possible, to ensure people feel a bit better about offering insights. Also, it helps immensely to create a comprehensive communications campaign around the survey, letting colleagues know why it's being done, who is conducting it, and why they can trust you to keep their data safe.

If you are successful in conducting a survey with high response rates that indicates where the organizational culture could use improvement, that's a great win. But don't stop there! Set up a meeting to share the data with a subset of senior-level leaders. This will open up an important window of opportunity for addressing culture at scale. Most leaders will be surprised and want to act on it.

However, most leaders won't know how! This is new territory. If there isn't an immediate action step taken, that window of opportunity could soon close. When presenting the data, make sure to include a "Call to Action" slide that suggests strategies leaders can use to address the problems.

You can improve chances of leadership buy-in (and, by the way, model another Human-Centered Leadership strategy) by providing a short menu of options that leaders can choose from. Just make sure they are relatively small and easy to implement. Remember that even institutions need to learn how to crawl before they can walk.

If you aren't sure what to put on your short list of potential solutions to the problem, here are a few ideas to get you started:

a. *Create an Action Task Force:* Work with leaders to identify a subset of employees and leaders whose main objective is to take action on culture and improve survey rates by the following year.
b. *Conduct a Pilot:* Try out a Human-Centered Leadership Workshop Series for a subset of managers as a test case for one part of the agency. Collect data to see if managers, as a result, are better able to create high-performing teams and improve culture.
c. *Hire a Director of Employee Experience and Engagement:* Make it someone's full-time duty to focus on how to transform the employee experience so that everyone feels empowered. (Just make sure the person has the resources to support the ideas described.)

3. Invite Me to Host a Book Talk in Your Institution!

It's sometimes hard to motivate action from the inside when you are on your own. By inviting an external resource person to your organization to do a book talk, you can quickly generate buzz and new energy around the topic. This strategy is also effective in identifying and creating connection with other employees passionate about the topic. That benefits you in discovering potential champions for the work, builds community, and initiates momentum—the precursors to change. Obviously, you can also invite other leaders on the topic! It doesn't have to be me.

(Strategies for Front-line Workers and Non-Supervisory Employees.)

4. Start a Book Club at Work

Book clubs aren't exclusive to chill time with your friends on Tuesday nights. They can also offer powerful opportunities to bring colleagues at work together to discuss important ideas that affect the workplace. The process for starting a book club is much the same at work as it is at home. Just ask a handful of friends and colleagues (especially those who you wish you spent more time with) if they'd like to join you in reading through the book. Find dates that work for everyone, a place to meet, who is bringing the cheese plate, and voila! You'll be initiating important dialogue for the institution while also increasing the number of meaningful connections you have with people you adore. And, who knows? Perhaps it will lead to something more.

If you want to widen the number of people who can participate, instead of a book club, you can facilitate a Brown-Bag Lunch on the topic and invite anyone who indicates an interest in joining.

5. Employee Resource Group (ERG) on Human-Centered Leadership

If your organization is already supporting ERGs, consider initiating a group focused on Human-Centered Leadership. The group can read the book together as fodder and then discuss strategies to support positive culture change in the organization. Or skip the book reading and go straight to discussing strategies to support change in your institution! The fact that your group is an ERG may provide access to leaders in ways you might not have been able to accomplish alone. In addition, you'll have a platform to bring like-minded employees together. That alone creates a deeper sense of joy and belonging.

Beyond Government (Implications for Corporations and NGOs)

If you've read this entire book, it may have occurred to you that most of the problems identified, and indeed most of the promising solutions for those problems, occur not just in government but in all workplace settings. That's because corporations, NGOs, and all types of workplace environments include managers and leaders who use the "old" kind of power. They genuinely believe that strong top-down leadership, compliance culture, and punitive mindsets are the only ways to motivate employees.

These managers have not done anything improper. The problem is that they haven't yet been exposed to the types of Human-Centered strategies that are described in this book. Most don't even know there are other leadership methods available to them. And when they learn that there are other ways to motivate employees, using methods that at the same time build trust, innovation, equity, and belonging, a fair portion of them will be open to trying it out. Those people create the entry point for wide-scale change.

No matter what type of institution, Human-Centered Leadership provides a concrete destination point for positive change that people from all walks of life can get behind. It offers the vehicle to realize that change through the development of skills and the implementation of strategies that create more space for each other on the journey. All we need now are a small group of committed individuals willing to be the fuel that gets the journey started.

Final Thoughts

If you had a magic wand, and could create the most inspiring workplace possible, what would it look like? Would all employees feel empowered to take initiative to solve problems, instead of them always sending it up the chain? Would collaboration across offices feel joyful and easy, in lieu of the turf wars and attack politics that too often thwart good work? And would all employees feel included and cherished in a space of belonging that they are proud to be a part of, rather than just showing up for the paycheck?

If the answer is yes, then Human-Centered Leadership might be for you. It doesn't take a lot of money. It's simply a reorganization of resources that you have already, so teams are working smarter, not harder.

But it also requires that leaders start from the heart. Sure, that may sound cheesy to some. Or to wishy-washy to others. But if there's only one takeaway from this book, there is nothing wishy-washy about Human-Centered Leadership.

Rather, this is about a new, concrete method of management that fosters the type of environment where all employees thrive at the highest possible level, creating the most good for the most people, and enabling institutions to flourish at their highest possible potential. It's about creating the infrastructure to catapult innovation, equity, and belonging.

Human-Centered Leadership does not need people to change their jobs, or even modify their duties. It just requires a small shift in mindset and a slightly new way of leading.

Rather than focusing leadership energy on telling, it focuses in on listening. Rather than using compliance and punishment as motivators for performance, it creates the conditions for employees to become self-motivated. Rather than being afraid to have conversations about equity, it establishes an environment for productive conversations that produce positive results and while making everyone feel valued.

It's a slight turn away from the more bold and unapologetic leadership style that some in government agencies are used to. It's a more nuanced type of management method. And when it is used well, it leads to bigger and better results for employees and institutions. And all it requires is the willingness to use Human-Centered Leadership as an entry point.

Resources & Opportunities

Those seeking additional resources to support culture-building efforts, check out the CenterforTransformingCulture.com.

To have your story considered for inclusion in future writings on Human-Centered Leadership go to:
CenterforTransformingCulture.com/share-your-story

End Notes

[1] Technically, the term 'fight or flight' has been expanded to include more responses. One fuller description includes fight, flight, freeze or appease.

[2] Clifton, J. (2017) "The World's Broken Workplace." Gallup.

[3] Twaronite, K. (2016) "A global survey on the ambiguous state of employee trust. Harvard Business Review.

[4] Unseem, J. (2017) "Power Causes Brain Damage." The Atlantic.

[5] Fisher, J. (2019) "How to get a job often comes down to one elite personal asset, and many people still don't realize it." CNBC

[6] Carr, E. (2019) "The value of belonging at work". Harvard Business Review.

[7] What is Dotmocracy (2021).

[8] To include more groups, just aggregate all the votes and take notes on the discussion from each group.

[9] Weighted polling offers the opportunity for people to vote on more than one option, weighting the answers based on what is most valued to them. For example, one person with five sticky dots can put each dot on five different answers. Another could put all five on one answer. And another could put two dots on one answer, and three on another. And so on.

[10] Foot, C. & Atkinson, R. "Federal Support for R&D Continues its Ignominious Slide" Information Technology and Innovation Foundation.

[11] Lawler, D. (2021) "America's Vaccination Rollout is Among the Best in the World" Axios – World.

[12] Tedx Talks. Edmondson, A. (2014) "Building a psychologically safe workplace" [Video]. YouTube.

[13] Donovan, R. et. al (2020) "Measuring Psychological Safety in Healthcare Teams". BMC Medical Research Methodology

Nembhard IM, et. al. (2006) "Making it safe: the effects of leader inclusiveness and professional status on psychological safety and improvement efforts in health care teams." Journal of Organizational Behavior.

Thygeson, N. (2021) Relational interventions for organizational learning. Learning Health Systems.

[14] Redford, G. (2019) "Amy Edmondson: Psychological Safety is Critically Important in Medicine." Association of American Medical Colleges.

[15] Williams, M. (2021) "Unsealed Archives Reveal Cover Ups at Chernobyl Plant Before Disaster." Reuters.

[16] Wang, V. (2021) "Chinese Citizen Journalist Sentenced to 4 Years for COVID Reporting." New York Times.

[17] The term 'women' here is inclusive of all persons who identify as women.

[18] The term "fight or flight" has been expanded to a larger scope. Some now call it "fight, flight, freeze, and appease". But we use the term a lot in this book, so we are going to use the original term to keep things concise. The term "fight or flight" has been expanded to a larger scope. Some now call it "fight, flight, freeze, and appease".

[19] Tabrizi, B. (2014) "The Key to Change is Middle Management" Harvard Business Review.

[20] Johnson, A. (2021) "Lack of Health Services and Transportation Impeded Access to Vaccine in Communities of Color". Washington Post.

Gould, E. et. al (2020) "Black Workers Face Two of the Most Lethal Pre-existing Conditions for Coronavirus - Racism and Economic Inequality". Economic Policy Institute

[21] Estrada, S. (2020) "D&I Roles Have More Than Doubled Since 2015". HR Drive.

[22] Crockett, E. (2016) "The Amazing Tool that Women in the White House Used to Fight Gender Bias".

[23] Goleman, D. (2004) "What Makes a Leader". Harvard Business Review.

Neale, P. (2020) "Emotional Intelligence: Why We Need It More Than Ever". Forbes Magazine

[24] Goleman, D. (2004) "What Makes a Leader". Harvard Business Review.

[25] Leadership traits are described as listed in the study. Descriptions have been provided to make concepts reader friendly.

[26] Conant, D. & Covey, S. (2016) "The Connection Between Employee Trust and Financial Performance".

[27] Conant, D. & Covey, S. (2016) "The Connection Between Employee Trust and Financial Performance".

[28] Schwabel, D. (2014) "Richard Branson: His 3 Most Important Leadership Principles". Forbes Magazine.

[29] Satelle, G. (2014) "Why Experts Always Seem to Get It Wrong". Forbes Magazine.

[30] Boschma, J. (2017) "Why Women Don't Run for Office. Politico".

[31] Chin, J. (2019) "Why Aren't There More Women Leaders". Psychology Today.

[32] Serwer, A. (2018) "The Cruelty Is The Point". The Atlantic.

[33] Wakefield, M. (2020) "How Narcissists Use DARVO to Escape Accountability". Medium.

[34] Barker, E. (2016) "How to Deal with a Narcissist. 5 Secrets Backed by Research".

[35] Ward, L. M., & Aubrey, J. S. (2017). "Watching gender: How stereotypes in movies and on TV impact kids' development". San Francisco, CA: Common Sense.

[36] Chamorro-Premuzic, T. (2019) "Attractive People Get Unfair Advantages at Work". Harvard Business Review.

[37] Dittmann, M. (2004) "Standing Tall Pays Off, Study Finds". American Psychological Association.

[38] Arends, B. (2020) "Americans Over 40 Are Half as Likely to Get Hired". Market Watch.

[39] Gerdeman, D. (2017) "Minorities Who Whiten Job Resumes Get More Interviews". Harvard Business School Weekly.

[40] Reiners, B. (2021) "16 Unconscious Bias Examples and How to Avoid Them in the Workplace". Builtin Website.

[41] Barken, R. (2014) "James to DeBlasio: Fire the Human Rights Commissioner". Observer.

[42] Originally said by first century Jewish scholar Hillel the Elder, and used by multiple U.S. presidents including John F. Kennedy, Ronald Reagan and Barack Obama.

About the Author

Dara Barlin is a shameless instigator for positive change. She has over two decades of experience in conducting research to inform policy, facilitating trust-building conversations, and organizing grassroots movements for a better world.

Her research has been featured in the U.S. Congress, United Nations, Institute for Public Policy Research, and Harvard Education Spotlight Series. Her campaigns for policy change have been touted as outstanding models by White House leaders, state legislators and human rights activists around the planet. In 2012, she led a global campaign that helped to build trust and develop a blueprint for collective progress across 97 countries. In response to the mental health crisis spurred on by the COVID-19 pandemic, Dara initiated a campaign to bring more effective communication skills to households around the world through gamification.

Dara has a master's degree with honors in Public Policy from the London School of Economics, and graduated Magna Cum Laude from Barnard College of Columbia University.

You can follow Dara on Facebook @Dara Barlin, Instagram @daremedara, Tik Tok @Dara.Barlin, or LinkedIn.